CAPITOL
HILL
COOKS

CAPITOL HILL COOKS

RECIPES from the WHITE HOUSE, CONGRESS, and All of the PAST PRESIDENTS

LINDA BAUER

3 1336 08755 3765

TAYLOR TRADE PUBLISHING

Lanham • New York • Boulder • Toronto • Plymouth, UK

Published by Taylor Trade Publishing
An imprint of The Rowman & Littlefield Publishing Group, Inc.
4501 Forbes Boulevard, Suite 200, Lanham, Maryland 20706
http://www.rlpgtrade.com

Estover Road, Plymouth PL6 7PY, United Kingdom

Distributed by National Book Network

British Library Cataloguing in Publication Information Available

Library of Congress Cataloging-in-Publication Data

Bauer, Linda.
  Capitol Hill cooks : recipes from the White House, Congress, and all of the past presidents /
Linda Bauer.
    p. cm.
  Includes index.
  ISBN 978-1-58979-550-1 (cloth : alk. paper) — ISBN 978-1-58979-569-3 (electronic)
  1. Cookery, American. 2. Cookery, American — history. I. Title.
  TX715.B3492 2010
  641.5973—dc22
                        2010001813

♾™ The paper used in this publication meets the minimum requirements of
American National Standard for Information Sciences—Permanence of
Paper for Printed Library Materials, ANSI/NISO Z39.48–1992.

Printed in the United States of America

To my mother, who passed away over fifteen years ago. Her unselfish dedication to others is still an inspiration for me each day. She was a strong proponent of selfless service and would have loved to help our troops through this exciting cookbook.

To my husband, Steve, a retired U.S. Army colonel, who knows the value and price of sacrifice and service to his country. To my father-in-law, Col. Elmer Bauer, and my uncle, Col. Bob Emrich, relatives who valiantly served our country and have gone to their reward. To Capt. Aaron Brown, may you be safe and happy.

To the military families, who are the backbone of love and support for our troops.

To our sons, Michael and Christopher, the lights of my life, may you never have to lose your lives and limbs in the fight for freedom, but never forget those who do.

To all of the troops who benefit from this particular book. May they find comfort in the support of those who love them and pray for them each day. Please support Homes for our Troops.

To the many volunteers who help to build homes for the brave men and women who fight for our country—thank you!!

Contents

★

Foreword

The first *American Sampler Cookbook* started literally as a dream to fight world hunger. It became a reality with the help of former senator Howard Metzenbaum, former congressman John Kasich of Ohio, and President and Mrs. Ronald Reagan. The kind cooperation of dedicated statesmen and their families created a beautiful book that helped the Red Cross in its endeavors.

The second version of the book, *The New American Sampler Cookbook*, was written during the presidency of George H. W. Bush. This collection aided World Vision in establishing programs worldwide to help bring water and food to those in need.

The third effort, *The Great American Sampler Cookbook*, fulfilled a cause that I fervently share with Barbara and Laura Bush: stamping out illiteracy. If such a task were accomplished, just imagine how many other problems could be solved at the same time.

Capitol Hill Cooks is the latest and best overall collection, containing not only the favorites of Congress but also the tasty treats enjoyed by our presidents from George Washington to Barack Obama! Hopefully your family will enjoy many of the over two hundred recipes from our statesmen plus almost one hundred recipes from our previous presidents. The recipes represent food from every corner of America.

The love of great cuisine and the bounty of our nation are evident in each and every recipe. Many contributors chose to relate tales of their ethnic backgrounds, favorite indigenous foods, and fond memories of meals shared with others.

Enjoy, and may God continue to bless America!

Acknowledgments

★

Special thanks to President and Mrs. Barack Obama, Vice President and Mrs. Joseph Biden, members of Congress, and their families for their extremely generous contributions to this book. Thanks to the presidential libraries, chefs, and past first families, who were so diligent in helping with the historic aspect of this book. Their dedication to the effort to help Homes for Our Troops was most encouraging. Special thanks to Mimi Neaman, my friend, and a genius with a heart of gold. To Rick Rinehart, a remarkable publisher; Elaine; Kalen; and all of the fine folks at Rowman & Littlefield for their extraordinary talent, professionalism, and altruism.

This cookbook aims to raise awareness of the plight of our troops who are disabled and need homes. I chose Homes for Our Troops because of its very high rating by Charity Navigator, a terrific resource to judge a charity's use of funds. If you wish to donate additional funds for these causes, please feel free to contact them directly.

Homes for Our Troops is a nonprofit, nonpartisan, 501(c)(3) organization founded in 2004. This organization is strongly committed to helping those who have selflessly given to their country and have returned home with serious disabilities and injuries. It assists severely injured servicemen and servicewomen and their immediate families by raising donations of money, building materials, and professional labor and then coordinating the process of building a new home or adapting an existing home for handicapped accessibility. The finished home is then given to the veteran.

Homes for Our Troops provides all services at no cost to the veterans and has been named a Top-Rated Charity by the American Institute of Philanthropy (AIP).

September 11, 2001, was a life-changing experience for all Americans. The resulting military deployments for Operation Iraqi

Freedom and, subsequently, Operation Enduring Freedom have profoundly changed the lives of many American service members.

After seeing a news story about a soldier who lost both of his legs in Iraq, John Gonsalves, a construction supervisor from Raynham, Massachusetts, wondered what was being done to support these men and women who had sacrificed so much for our country. He set out on a mission to join in the effort to build specially adapted housing and modify and retrofit homes for those most severely injured. Not finding any organization that was supporting such a mission, he knew that he needed to do something to help these American heroes. Traveling to visit with wounded veterans, speaking with veterans' organizations, and researching the difficulties facing America's injured service members as they tried to find specially adapted and barrier-free homes, John realized most handicapped housing did not take into consideration the types of disabilities incurred in combat. In February 2004, John founded Homes for Our Troops.

> Starting up a nonprofit organization was an area as far away from supervising construction projects as it gets. It's been a learning experience, and so rewarding. The outpouring of generous citizens at times is overwhelming. The veterans I have met along the way have touched my heart, and I am honored to have them as my friends. Homes for Our Troops is dedicated to building specially adapted homes for disabled veterans, as long as there is a need.
>
> —John Gonsalves

Gonsalves is committed to running the nonprofit organization by maintaining the highest professional standards and keeping it financially efficient and professionally staffed with dedicated personnel. His efforts were recently rewarded when the AIP, one of the country's premier charity watchdog organizations, reviewed Homes for Our Troops' finances and included the organization in their Top-Rated Veterans & Military Charities listing with an "A" rating. Charity Navigator recently awarded Homes for Our Troops with a four-star rating, the highest rating available.

Homes for Our Troops built a handful of homes in its first two years as it worked diligently to spread the word nationwide about its mission in order to raise funds to meet the great need for hundreds of specially adapted homes for our most severely injured American heroes. Since then, Homes for Our Troops has grown into a highly rated, prominent, national nonprofit organization that had built more than three dozen homes by the end of 2008. In 2009 there were about thirty more homes in the build process.

Gonsalves travels extensively throughout the United States speaking about Homes for Our Troops and advocating on behalf of injured veterans, including testifying before the House Committee on Veterans Affairs, Subcommittee on Economic Opportunity Hearing on Specialty Adapted Housing.

He has been featured in the national media, including on CNN, *NBC Nightly News*, Fox News, and numerous local media outlets across the country.

Awards and Recognitions

Office of the Secretary of Defense Medal for Exceptional Public Service

Ellis Island Medal of Honor

Ellis Island Medal of Honor Society Member

Quoted by President George W. Bush in his address to the troops at Camp Pendleton, California

Daughters of the American Revolution Medal of Honor

ENR Top 25 Newsmakers Award

Home Magazine's Home Shelter Award

Meeting with President and Mrs. George W. Bush in the Oval Office

Massachusetts National Guard Minuteman Award

Gonsalves has also received letters of support from the president of the United States, members of Congress, senators and governors and high-ranking military officials, including Senator Edward Kennedy, former deputy secretary of defense Paul Wolfowitz, and Maj. Gen. William B. Caldwell of the U.S. Army.

Mailing Address

Homes for Our Troops
6 Main Street
Taunton, MA 02780
Phone: (508) 823-3300
Toll-free: (866) 7 TROOPS
Fax: (508) 823-5411
www.homesforourtroops.org

To contact Gonsalves about corporate sponsorship opportunities, e-mail him at john@homesforourtroops.org

To contact the author for speaking engagements (especially to raise funds for veterans, library, or literacy organizations), write to bauerbooks@gmail.com.

APPETIZERS

★ 1

Dips, Pâtés,
Hors d'oeuvres,
and First Courses

MARGE'S CHILE CON QUESO DIP

Senator Tom Udall, NEW MEXICO

1	pound Swiss cheese, cubed
32	ounces tomato sauce
8 to 10	hot green chilies, roasted and diced
2	tablespoons garlic salt

Mix all ingredients together in a saucepan over low heat. If mixture appears too thick, add a little more tomato sauce. *Do not mix a lot*; stir occasionally.

When cheese is completely melted, eat with plain tortilla chips.

A New Mexico classic loved by everyone. *Buen provecho!*

PICNIC PÂTÉ

Senator Christopher Bond, MISSOURI

4 tablespoons butter
½ pound fresh mushrooms
4 green onions, minced
4 tablespoons sherry
8 ounces liverwurst
16 ounces cream cheese, softened
1 teaspoon fresh dill, chopped
1 teaspoon fresh chervil, chopped
2 teaspoons Dijon mustard
Salt and freshly ground pepper to taste

Melt butter in a skillet. Sauté mushrooms and green onions until soft. Stir in sherry.
Cool.

Place mushroom mixture and remaining ingredients in a food processor or blender. Process until very smooth. Transfer to a crock or serving bowl.

Refrigerate for at least 24 hours before serving. Garnish with sprigs of fresh dill. Serve with party rye and a selection of pickles.

Makes 12 servings.

Mushrooms are the magic in this savory pâté. Tuck it away in a picnic basket along with a hefty supply of sandwiches, pickles, and fresh fruit and enjoy an outing under the Gateway Arch.

EASTER EGG DIP

Senator Christopher Bond, MISSOURI

- 2 tablespoons lemon juice
- 1 tablespoon onion juice
- 1 teaspoon coarse ground mustard
- 2 teaspoons mustard
- ½ cup mayonnaise
- ½ teaspoon Tabasco sauce
- 6 hard-cooked eggs, chopped
- ½ teaspoon seasoned salt
- ¼ teaspoon white pepper
- 4 ounces olive-and-pimento cream cheese, whipped
  Fresh parsley or dill, chopped

In a mixer or blender, combine juices, mustards, mayonnaise, and Tabasco sauce. Add eggs one by one, beating after each addition until smooth and light.

Beat in salt, pepper, and cream cheese. Turn into chilled bowl, smooth top, and garnish with chopped fresh parsley or dill. Serve with crudités (raw vegetables) or assorted crackers. May be spread on bread for tea sandwiches.

Makes 2 cups.

Reviving an old tradition, we hosted our first Easter egg hunt on the lawn of the Missouri Governor's Mansion in 1973. Since our son, Sam, arrived, the hunt has become an annual event. This unusual dip proved the perfect solution for leftover Easter eggs.

CURRY CAPER DIP

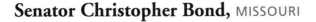

Senator Christopher Bond, MISSOURI

1   cup mayonnaise
½   cup sour cream
1   teaspoon crushed herbs, such as basil, thyme,
     or oregano
¼   teaspoon salt
⅛   teaspoon curry
1   tablespoon onion, grated
1   tablespoon fresh parsley, chopped
1½   teaspoons lemon juice
2   teaspoons capers, drained
½   teaspoon Worcestershire sauce

Mix all ingredients. Chill. Serve with crudités (raw vegetables). For a colorful presentation, spoon the dip into a hollowed-out red cabbage or eggplant.

Makes 1½ cups.

My favorite dip for raw vegetables always recalls memories of the good friend who parted with this gem.

MUSTARD SAUCE

★

Senator Charles Grassley, IOWA

4 tablespoons dry mustard

1 tablespoon butter

¼ cup water

6 tablespoons sugar

6 tablespoons apple cider vinegar

1 egg, beaten

Make a paste of the dry mustard, butter, and water. Add sugar and vinegar. Bring to a boil. Temper the beaten egg into the boiling liquid.

Cook until thick. Refrigerate. Pour over an 8-ounce block of cream cheese. Serve with crackers.

Makes 20 servings.

We've enjoyed this treat with Sue, a former Des Moines girl. Her backyard adjoins ours.

CHEESE BALL

Senator Charles Grassley, IOWA

16 ounces cream cheese, softened
1 package Good Seasons Italian salad dressing mix,
   dry
1 cup pecans, chopped

Mix cream cheese, salad dressing mix, and ½ cup chopped nuts. Shape into 2 balls and roll in the remaining chopped pecans. Makes 24 servings.

Best if made a little ahead so flavors can blend. Serve with crackers.

FIESTA CHEESE WHEEL

Senator Christopher Bond, MISSOURI

14½	ounces whole plum tomatoes, drained and diced
8	ounces cream cheese, softened
8	ounces cheddar cheese, grated
½	cup butter softened
½	cup onion, finely chopped
2	cloves garlic, crushed
1	teaspoon salt
¼	teaspoon cayenne pepper
⅛	teaspoon ground cumin
¾	cup walnuts, chopped
2	tablespoons fresh parsley, chopped

Seed tomatoes and dry between paper towels. Combine tomatoes, cream cheese, cheddar cheese, butter, onion, garlic, salt, cayenne pepper, and cumin. Beat until smooth with an electric mixer.

Spoon mixture onto a large piece of waxed paper. Shape into a wheel approximately 1" thick. Chill until firm.

Cover wheel with chopped walnuts. Sprinkle with parsley.

Serve as an appetizer with crackers or tortilla chips.

Makes 20 servings.

> Great for a tailgate party before a Cardinals or Chiefs game.

SWEET AND SOUR MEATBALLS

★

Senator Christopher Bond, MISSOURI

MEATBALLS

5	pounds ground chuck
1	pound ground pork
4	eggs
4	teaspoons salt
2	teaspoons pepper
1	teaspoon nutmeg
3	tablespoons seasoning salt
2	cups light cream
1	large onion, finely chopped
12	ounces bread crumbs

SWEET AND SOUR SAUCE

52	ounces (4 cans) chunked pineapple
½	cup cornstarch
1	cup red wine vinegar
2	cups brown sugar
¼	cup soy sauce
1	green pepper, finely diced

MEATBALLS

Combine all meatball ingredients. Shape mixture into balls about
1" in diameter. Brown in vegetable oil and cook thoroughly. Drain,
cool, and refrigerate.

Makes 9 dozen.

SAUCE

Drain pineapple, retaining juice. Add enough water to juice to make
4 cups. Dissolve cornstarch in vinegar. Combine all ingredients,

(continued)

except green pepper. Cook, stirring constantly, until thickened. Add green pepper. Heat thoroughly. To serve, heat meatballs in sauce. Transfer to a chafing dish.

We were still newlyweds when I ran for the U.S. Congress in 1968, and our first parade of that campaign was during the Hermann Maifest. Following the event, we were invited to a reception where these savory meatballs were served. Featuring pork and soy, two of Missouri's major agricultural products, they are always a popular item on a buffet table.

ALASKA SALMON DIP Á LA LISA

Senator Lisa Murkowski, ALASKA

8 ounces (1 package) cream cheese, softened
½ cup sour cream
1 tablespoon fresh lemon juice
1 tablespoon fresh dill, minced
1 teaspoon prepared horseradish
½ teaspoon kosher salt
¼ teaspoon freshly ground pepper
4 ounces Alaska salmon, smoked

Cream the cheese until smooth. Add sour cream, lemon juice, dill, horseradish, salt, and pepper.

Mix well. Add smoked salmon, mixing well.

Chill and serve with crudités (raw vegetables) or crackers.

CHIP DIP

★

Senator Benjamin Nelson, NEBRASKA

5 to 7 ounces (1 can) of shrimp, drained and rinsed
        or 1 cup fresh cooked shrimp, medium sized
  ½ cup chili sauce
  8 ounces cream cheese, softened
  ½ cup mayonnaise
  ¼ cup onion, chopped
  2 teaspoons horseradish

Blend chili sauce into cream cheese.
Mix in rest of ingredients. Add shrimp carefully. Chill until ready to serve.

CHEESY FIESTA DIP

★

Senator Michael Enzi, WYOMING

  1 pound lean hamburger, browned and drained
 14 ounces refried beans
  4 ounces green chilies
  1 10-ounce can of tomatoes
  2 pounds Velveeta processed cheese, cut into small
    cubes

Combine the hamburger, refried beans, chilies, and tomatoes, and place into a crock pot.

Heat on a low setting. Add cheese cubes and stir frequently to mix.

Serve with tortilla chips and fresh vegetables.

SALADS

 2

HEALTHY COLD TURKEY SALAD

★

Senator Barbara Boxer, CALIFORNIA

SALAD

    2   cups cooked white turkey meat, cubed

    ¼   cup sweet red onion, chopped

    ½   cup red or yellow bell pepper, chopped

    ½   cup water chestnuts or jicama, chopped

    ¼   cup walnuts, chopped

        Freshly ground pepper to taste

DRESSING

    ¼   cup yogurt

    ¼   cup light mayonnaise

    1   teaspoon dill weed

    ¼   cup parsley, minced

    1   tablespoon lemon juice

        Salt to taste

Mix salad ingredients and toss lightly. Combine dressing ingredients and pour over salad. Chill.
Makes 6 servings.

CURRIED CHICKEN SALAD

★

Senator Christopher Bond, MISSOURI

2 cups cooked chicken breasts, diced
4 scallions, sliced
1 cup water chestnuts, sliced
2 cups cooked rice, room temperature
1 cup mayonnaise
½ cup prepared chutney
1 teaspoon curry powder
1 teaspoon salt
2 bananas
¼ cup lemon juice
1½ cups peanuts, chopped
Freshly ground pepper to taste

Combine chicken, scallions, and water chestnuts with rice. In a separate bowl, combine mayonnaise, chutney, curry powder, salt, and pepper. Add to chicken and rice mixture. Chill. Taste and adjust seasonings. Cut bananas diagonally into 1" slices. Dip slices in lemon juice and coat with peanuts.

To serve, arrange salad on small platter. Surround salad with banana slices and garnish with chopped nuts. Additional condiments may be served: chopped green peppers, toasted almonds, plumped raisins, and coconut are a few choices.

Makes 6 to 8 servings.

Following our son Sam's christening at the First Presbyterian Church in my hometown of Mexico, Missouri, this savory chicken salad was featured along with asparagus and a watermelon basket brimming with fresh fruit. That Father's Day in 1981 is a date we'll never forget.

PASTA SALAD

★

Senator Richard Lugar, INDIANA

1   pound spaghetti
1   green pepper
1   bunch green onions
2   stalks celery
2   tomatoes
1   cucumber
1   8-ounce bottle Italian dressing
1   bottle McCormick's Salad Supreme

B reak spaghetti into bite-sized pieces and cook. Chop vegetables finely. Drain pasta and add all other ingredients. Mix together while pasta is still warm.

Best when made a day ahead and refrigerated. Serve cold or at room temperature.

Makes 15 to 20 servings.

This is an ideal dish for a potluck supper.

SUMMER RICE SALAD

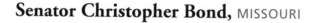

Senator Christopher Bond, MISSOURI

SALAD

3	cups cooked rice, cooled
¼	cup mayonnaise
½	cup radishes, thinly sliced
½	cup scallions, thinly sliced
1	sweet red pepper, minced
2	tablespoons sweet gherkins, minced
1	tablespoon fresh parsley, minced
1	tablespoon fresh dill, chopped
1	tablespoon fresh chives, snipped

The diversity of Missouri agriculture is possibly most apparent in the Boot Heel. In this southeast corner of the state, you will discover cotton and rice as well as the more typical corn and soybean crops. A barbecue in conjunction with the Sikeston Cotton Carnival yielded this summer sensation.

DRESSING

½	cup fresh lemon juice
2	teaspoons salt
2	garlic cloves, crushed
1¼	cups salad oil

Combine salad ingredients and mix well, then set aside. Place lemon juice, salt, and garlic in a food processor or blender and mix well. With machine running, add oil in a thin stream until thoroughly incorporated. (If added too quickly, dressing may separate.)

Add dressing to rice mixture and season with salt and pepper. Taste and adjust seasoning.

Refrigerate and allow to return to room temperature before serving. Mound on lettuce leaves and garnish with black olives or red pepper rings.

Makes 8 to 10 servings.

MARINATED VEGETABLE SALAD

Representative Ike Skelton, MISSOURI

MARINADE

½ cup apple cider vinegar

¼ cup sugar

1 cup vegetable or olive oil

2 cloves garlic, pressed with garlic press or mashed

½ cup red wine vinegar

1 teaspoon dry mustard

2 teaspoons salt

1 tablespoon dried oregano leaves, crushed

1 teaspoon pepper

1 8-ounce bottle Italian dressing

VEGETABLES

2 green peppers, thinly sliced

1 cucumber, thinly sliced

1 head cauliflower, broken into florets

6 carrots, thinly sliced

1 pound fresh mushrooms, sliced

5 stalks celery, sliced

1 bunch green onions, sliced

1 dozen cherry tomatoes, halved

MARINADE

Bring apple cider vinegar to boil. Add sugar and oil; stir until sugar dissolves. Let mixture cool. Add all remaining marinade ingredients.

VEGETABLES

Place all prepared vegetables in a large noncorrosive bowl or wide-mouthed jar. Pour marinade over the vegetables. Cover with plastic wrap.

Refrigerate for 24 hours. Stir or turn mixture at least 3 or 4 times during the 24-hour period. To serve, drain vegetables and place in a clear glass bowl.

Makes 20 servings.

GREEK SALAD

Representative Mike Bilirakis, FLORIDA

DRESSING

½ cup olive oil

½ cup red wine vinegar

1 teaspoon salt

¼ teaspoon pepper

½ teaspoon sugar

1 clove garlic, crushed

1 teaspoon dried oregano leaves

> This is a traditional Greek salad that our family and friends have enjoyed for many years.

SALAD

1 small head lettuce

1 medium tomato, sliced

1 medium cucumber, sliced

3 green onions, chopped

1 small green pepper, cut into strips

¾ cup Feta cheese, cut into cubes or crumbled

Greek black olives

Greek hot salad peppers (from a jar)

Anchovy fillets, chopped (optional)

DRESSING

Combine all dressing ingredients in a jar or cruet. Shake until thoroughly blended. Prepare well in advance and keep refrigerated until ready to use. Makes 1 cup. Shake well before using.

SALAD

To prepare salad, break lettuce in small pieces. Place in salad bowl with tomato, cucumber, onion, and green pepper. Top with Feta cheese, black olives, hot salad peppers, and anchovy fillets if desired. Pour dressing over salad and serve.

Makes 4 servings.

ORANGE CHICKEN SALAD

★

Senator Michael Enzi, WYOMING

SALAD

6	cups iceberg lettuce, cut into bite-sized pieces
22	ounces (2 cans) mandarin oranges, drained
3	green onions, sliced thin
¾	cup celery, diced
12½	ounces (1 can) white chicken, packed in water, drained
¾	cup slivered almonds (optional)

HONEY-MUSTARD DRESSING

¾	cup olive oil
⅓	cup apple cider vinegar or lemon juice
6	tablespoons honey
1	teaspoon garlic salt
1	teaspoon dry mustard
½ to 1	teaspoon dill weed

In a large bowl, toss the salad ingredients until well mixed.

Blend dressing ingredients. Add ½ cup dressing to salad. Toss again.

Serve over Chinese noodles.

Makes 6 servings.

HOT CHICKEN SALAD

Senator Robert Bennett, UTAH

⅔ cup slivered almonds

4 cups cooked chicken, diced (about 6 large breasts)

2 tablespoons lemon juice

¾ cup mayonnaise

2 cups celery, finely chopped

1 cup cream of chicken soup

1 teaspoon onion, minced

1 cup cheddar cheese, grated

1½ cups potato chips or cornflakes

Toast almonds on a cookie sheet in a 350 degree oven for 5 to 7 minutes. (Watch carefully.)

Mix all ingredients except cheese and potato chips. Add cheese to top of mixture, followed by chips.

Bake at 400 degrees for 20 minutes.

Makes 4 to 6 servings.

NAPA SALAD

Senator Sam Brownback, KANSAS

SALAD

    1 head Napa cabbage

    6 green onions

    2 packages Ramen noodles, flavor packet removed

    4 ounces slivered almonds

    4 ounces sunflower seeds, unsalted

    ½ cup butter or margarine

DRESSING

    2 tablespoons soy sauce

    1 cup sugar

    ½ cup tarragon vinegar

    1 cup sunflower oil

SALAD

Dice cabbage and onions. Mix together then refrigerate for at least 2 hours. Break apart Ramen noodles.

Put noodles, almonds, sunflower seeds, and butter in skillet and sauté until slightly brown. Refrigerate. Combine cabbage mixture and noodle mixture 2 hours before serving.

DRESSING

Mix together soy sauce, sugar, vinegar, and oil. Pour over salad 15 minutes before serving. Stir. Serve.

Makes 4 servings.

SOUTHWEST POTATO SALAD

★

Representative John Boehner, OHIO

10 to 14 large red potatoes, washed and unpeeled
2 cups mayonnaise or salad dressing
1 medium ripe tomato, chopped
½ green pepper, chopped
2 green onions, chopped
2 cloves garlic, minced
2 tablespoons fresh cilantro, chopped
1 tablespoon Dijon mustard
2 tablespoons lime juice
1 teaspoon salt
½ teaspoon pepper
½ teaspoon (or more to taste) cayenne pepper
1 pound bacon, fried and chopped (optional)
4 hard-cooked eggs (optional)

Place potatoes in pot and add cold water to cover by about 2". Bring to a boil and cook for 60 minutes or until potatoes are done.

While potatoes are cooking, combine remaining ingredients in a large bowl.

Allow cooked potatoes to cool enough to handle. Cut into sixths or eighths and add to dressing while still warm. Toss gently to coat.

Let stand at room temperature for 30 minutes before serving or refrigerate up to 2 days.

Makes 10 servings.

LAYERED SALAD

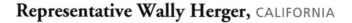

Representative Wally Herger, CALIFORNIA

SALAD

  1 medium head lettuce
  ½ cup green onions, thinly sliced
  1 cup celery, thinly sliced
  8 ounces water chestnuts, sliced
  10 ounces frozen peas

DRESSING

  2 cups mayonnaise
  ½ cup grated Parmesan cheese
  ¼ teaspoon garlic powder

GARNISH

  3 hard-cooked eggs, grated
  1 pound bacon, cooked and crumbled
  2 or 3 tomatoes, cut into wedges

Layer salad ingredients in the order listed. Top with dressing mixture.

Cover and chill up to 24 hours. Garnish before serving.

Makes 10 servings.

PRETZEL SALAD

Representative Chet Edwards, TEXAS

1	cup pretzels, crushed
½	cup butter
½	cup sugar
8	ounces (1 package) cream cheese, softened
8	ounces (1 tub) whipped topping
½	cup sugar
2	tablespoons cornstarch
¼	cup sugar
20	ounces crushed pineapple, drained, reserving liquid

Mix pretzels, butter, and sugar together and spread into an 8" × 12" dish. Bake crust 5 minutes at 350 degrees. Let cool. Mix cream cheese, whipped topping, and sugar. Spread over first layer.

Mix cornstarch, sugar, and pineapple juice drained from the can of crushed pineapple. Cook on stove over medium heat until thick. Let cool.

Stir in crushed pineapple.

Spread over second layer. Top with whipped topping. Chill.

Makes 12 to 15 servings.

SOUPS AND STEWS

★ 3

Soups, Chowders,
Stews, and Chilis

TORTILLA SOUP

★

Senator Tom Udall, NEW MEXICO

1 tablespoon onion, finely chopped
1 clove garlic, minced
2 tablespoons shortening
2 cups chicken stock or bouillon broth
   dissolved in 2 cups water
¼ teaspoon ground cumin
3 dried red chili pods, cleaned and cut in strips
1 cup longhorn, cheddar, or Swiss cheese, grated
   Corn chips
   Salt to taste

In a deep saucepan, sauté onion and garlic in shortening. Add stock, cumin, and salt. Add strips of chili and boil slowly until chili is tender.

Before serving, add grated cheese. Stir. Serve on half bowl of corn chips.

Makes 4 servings.

A soup to complement any meal.

UNITED STATES HOUSE OF REPRESENTATIVES BEAN SOUP

Representative Joe Barton, TEXAS

2 pounds number 1 Michigan beans
1 smoked ham hock
  Salt and pepper to taste

Cover beans with cold water and soak overnight.

Drain and cover with water again.

Add a smoked ham hock and simmer slowly for about 4 hours until beans are cooked and tender. Then add salt and pepper to taste. Just before serving, bruise beans with large spoon or ladle, enough to cloud.

Makes 6 servings.

Bean soup has been a featured item on the menu of the House of Representatives Restaurant since long before that day in 1904 when Speaker of the House Joseph G. Cannon of Illinois came into the House Restaurant and ordered bean soup.

Then, as now, bean soup was a hearty, zesty, and filling dish; but on that particular day in Washington, DC, it was hot and humid, and bean soup had therefore been omitted from the menu. "Thunderation," roared Speaker Cannon, "I had my mouth set for bean soup." He continued, "From now on, hot or cold, rain, snow or shine, I want it on the menu every day."

And so it has been—bean soup on the menu every single day since.

LENTIL BARLEY STEW

★

Representative Michael Castle, DELAWARE

¼ cup butter

⅓ cup onion, chopped

½ cup celery, chopped

1 pound stewed tomatoes

2 cups water

½ cup lentils, well rinsed

⅓ cup medium barley

¼ teaspoon rosemary, crushed

⅓ cup carrots, shredded

½ teaspoon salt

Dash of pepper

1 teaspoon sugar (optional)

Crushed red pepper (optional)

Melt butter in large heavy saucepan over moderate heat. Add onion and celery and cook until onion is lightly browned. Stir in tomatoes, water, lentils, barley, salt, pepper, and rosemary. Bring to a boil.

Cover tightly and boil gently for 25 minutes, stirring occasionally. Add carrots and cook 5 minutes longer.

May be frozen.

Makes 6 servings.

Please note: I add a teaspoon of sugar to reduce the acidity of the tomatoes. Also for a little zip, add a few shakes of crushed red pepper.

KAY'S SHADYWOOD SHOWDOWN CHILI

★

Senator Kay Bailey Hutchinson, TEXAS

2	medium yellow onions, diced
2	green peppers, diced
1	tablespoon olive oil
2½	pounds ground sirloin
¼	cup mole sauce
16	ounces (1 can) tomato sauce
4	cups water
¼	cup chili powder
	Salt and pepper to taste
	Garlic powder to taste
16	ounces (1 can) kidney beans (optional)

Sauté half of the onions and peppers in 1 tablespoon olive oil. Brown meat separately, leaving chunks. Drain fat. Add onion and pepper mixture to meat. Add 3 tablespoons mole sauce to mixture.

Transfer to large pot. Add tomato sauce, water, and 3 tablespoons chili powder. Bring to boil. Add remaining mole, if desired, and salt, pepper, and garlic powder to taste. Simmer 1 hour, stirring occasionally.

Sauté remaining onions and peppers. Add to pot, along with drained beans. Add final chili powder to taste.

Finish heating and serve with favorite fixings.

Makes 6 servings.

CAPE COD FISH CHOWDER

Representative Patrick Kennedy, RHODE ISLAND

- 2 pounds fresh haddock
- 2 ounces salt pork, diced (or 2 tablespoons butter or margarine)
- 2 medium onions, sliced
- 1 cup celery, chopped
- 4 large potatoes, diced
- 1 bay leaf, crumbled
- 1 quart milk
- 2 tablespoons butter or margarine
- 1 teaspoon salt
  Freshly ground pepper to taste

Simmer haddock in 2 cups of water for 15 minutes. Drain off and reserve broth. Remove skin and bones from fish.

Sauté diced salt pork in a large pot until crisp. Remove cooked salt pork. Sauté onions in pork fat or butter until golden brown. Add fish, celery, potatoes, and bay leaf.

Measure reserved fish broth plus enough boiling water to make 3 cups liquid. Add to pot and simmer for 30 minutes. Add milk and butter and simmer for an additional 5 minutes or until well heated. Add salt and pepper to taste.

Makes 8 servings.

Enjoy this hearty New England favorite of mine and my father's!

BACON AND BEAN CHOWDER

Senator Charles Grassley, IOWA

1   cup navy or pea beans, drained
1   quart water
6   slices bacon, diced
1   onion, chopped
2   teaspoons pepper
1⅓ cups potato, diced
1⅓ cups celery, including leaves, diced
1½ cups carrots, sliced
29 ounces (1 can) tomatoes
2   tablespoons flour
2   cups hot milk
    Dried parsley
    American cheese, grated

Combine beans and water in a large kettle. Bring to a boil and cook for 2 minutes. Remove from heat and let stand for 1 hour. Cook bacon and onion until lightly browned. Add, with fat, to beans.

Bring to a boil again. Cover and simmer for 1 hour. Add pepper, potato, celery, carrots, and tomatoes. Simmer 30 minutes longer.

Blend flour with a little cold water and stir into soup. Cook until slightly thickened. Add hot milk and additional seasoning, if necessary. Stir in dried parsley and cheese.

Makes about 2 quarts.

> Florence is one of the best cooks I know, and I'm sure that she won't mind sharing her recipe with you.

CURRIED PEA SOUP

Senator Christopher Bond, MISSOURI

10 ounces (1 package) frozen peas
1 medium onion, sliced
1 small carrot, sliced
1 rib of celery with leaves, sliced
1 medium potato, sliced
1 garlic clove, crushed
1 teaspoon salt
1 teaspoon curry powder
2 cups chicken stock, divided
1 cup heavy cream
  Mint leaves *or* 1 teaspoon sour cream
  Crumbled bacon

Place vegetables, seasonings, and 1 cup of stock in a saucepan and bring to a boil. Cover, reduce heat, and simmer 20 to 30 minutes until vegetables are very tender. Transfer vegetables to a food processor or blender. Puree. With the motor running, pour in remaining stock and the cream. Chill. Garnish each portion with whipped cream and a mint leaf.

To serve hot, omit adding cream in food processor or blender. Instead, process puree and stock only. Heat. Remove from heat and stir in cream. Garnish with a teaspoon of sour cream and crisply cooked, crumbled bacon.

Makes 4 to 6 servings.

WATERCRESS SOUP

Senator Christopher Bond, MISSOURI

6	cups watercress
3	tablespoons butter, divided
¼	cup onion, minced
1½	cups water
1	teaspoon salt
½	teaspoon white pepper
½	teaspoon curry powder
2	tablespoons flour
29	ounces (2 cans) chicken broth
2	cups milk
2	egg yolks
1	cup heavy cream

Rinse and drain watercress. Remove coarsest stems. Reserve. Melt 1 tablespoon butter in a large saucepan. Add onion and cook until golden. Add watercress, water, salt, pepper, and curry powder. Cook over high heat for 5 minutes.

Transfer mixture to a food processor or blender. Puree. Melt remaining 2 tablespoons butter in a saucepan and stir in flour. Add chicken broth and milk; bring to a boil. Stir in watercress mixture.

Combine egg yolks and heavy cream and beat until slightly thickened. Stir 1 cup of hot soup into egg and cream mixture. Add to remaining soup, stirring constantly. Heat, but do not boil. Garnish with croutons and a sprig of watercress.

Makes 8 servings.

While I fish for trout from the back of the canoe, my wife usually is at the bow searching for watercress. A fall float trip on the Eleven Point River yielded a bumper crop and led to the development of this refreshing soup. We enjoy it as a prelude to a light luncheon or patio supper.

POLISH SAUSAGE STEW

Senator Charles Grassley, IOWA

10½ ounces (1 can) cream of celery soup

⅓ cup light brown sugar

16 ounces (1 can) sauerkraut, drained

2 pounds Polish sausage, cut in chunks

4 medium potatoes, cubed

1 cup onion, chopped

1 cup Monterey Jack cheese, shredded

Combine in a crock pot the soup, sugar, and sauerkraut. Add the sausage, potatoes, and onion. Cook on low for 8 hours or on high for 4 hours. Skim off fat and stir in cheese just before serving.

Makes 4 to 6 servings.

Our friend Jolene brought this to our house for supper one night.

SAUSAGE ZUCCHINI SOUP

Senator Christopher Bond, MISSOURI

1¼ pounds mild Italian sausage without casings
1½ cups celery, sliced
 4 pounds fresh tomatoes, peeled and cut in wedges
1½ cups tomato juice
 1 teaspoon salt
1½ teaspoons Italian seasoning (or a mixture of basil
    and oregano)
 1 teaspoon sugar
 ¼ teaspoon garlic salt
 2 green peppers, cut into 1" pieces
1½ pounds zucchini, cut into ½" slices
 1 cup mozzarella cheese, shredded

Crumble sausage into a 4-quart saucepan; brown and drain fat. Add celery and cook 10 minutes. Add tomatoes, juice, and seasonings and simmer for 10 minutes. Stir in green peppers. Cook for 5 minutes.

Add zucchini and cook 1 to 2 minutes, until barely heated. *Caution:* Do not overcook zucchini. Sprinkle mozzarella cheese over the top.

Serve immediately.

Makes 8 to 10 servings.

Note: If more liquid is desired, add more tomato juice. Two 28-ounce cans of Italian plum tomatoes may be substituted for fresh tomatoes.

During a visit to Rolla for the annual St. Patrick's Day festivities, we sampled this substantial and satisfying soup at the home of a friend. Ladle into sizable soup bowls and serve in front of a crackling fire.

MISSOURI APPLE SOUP

Senator Christopher Bond, MISSOURI

2	tablespoons butter
2	medium onions, thinly sliced
6	red Jonathan apples, peeled, cored, and diced
4	cups chicken broth
2	tablespoons sugar
1	tablespoon curry powder
	Salt and freshly ground white pepper to taste
1 to 2	cups light cream
	Apple wedges
	Sliced almonds

In a Dutch oven, melt butter and sauté onions until transparent. Add apples, broth, sugar, and curry powder. Season with salt and pepper. Cook covered over low heat until apples are soft. Strain apples and onions from broth and reserve. Set broth aside.

Place apples and onions in a food processor or blender. Puree. Add broth and blend well. Add cream according to desired richness. Chill. Taste and adjust seasoning. Garnish with thin apple wedges and a sprinkling of sliced almonds.

Makes 10 to 12 servings.

Stephenson's Apple Orchard in eastern Jackson County is a name that brings to mind family outings during the fall picking season and bushel baskets heaping with succulent apples.

OYSTER STEW

Representative Howard Coble, NORTH CAROLINA

2 quarts whole milk
1 pint select oysters, shucked
2 tablespoons butter
Salt and pepper to taste

Combine all ingredients. Cook over low heat.
Heat to simmering, but do not boil. Serve piping hot with crackers.
  Makes 8 servings.
  Note: For a slightly thicker stew, stir 1 or 2 tablespoons flour into a small amount of milk until smooth. Add to pot and heat to piping hot.

> This dish is particularly tasty during the winter months and is particularly easy for us bachelors to prepare.

NEW ENGLAND
CLAM CHOWDER

★

Representative Paul Kanjorski, PENNSYLVANIA

¼	pound salt bacon
1	large Spanish onion, chopped
18 to 24	ounces (3 bottles) Doxsee clam juice
4	large potatoes, peeled and sliced
21	ounces whole baby clams
1½	quarts half-and-half
	Oyster crackers

Finely chop bacon and begin browning. Add onion and brown until clear.

Add clam juice, potatoes, and clams to mixture and heat until potatoes are tender.

Add half-and-half and heat until close to boiling. If necessary, add regular milk to dilute to desired consistency. Serve immediately with oyster crackers.

Makes 12 servings.

Note: Do not add half-and-half until ready to serve. Before milk is added, the mixture may even be refrigerated until serving time.

CAULIFLOWER SOUP

Senator Joseph Lieberman, CONNECTICUT

3 tablespoons butter or margarine
3 tablespoons flour
⅛ teaspoon nutmeg
3⅔ cups chicken broth
1 cup water
3 cups small cauliflowerets
1 egg yolk
3 tablespoons heavy cream
Snipped fresh parsley

In a medium saucepan, melt butter or margarine and blend in flour and nutmeg. Slowly stir in broth and water, then bring to a boil while stirring. Add cauliflowerets. Simmer soup, covered, about 25 minutes or until cauliflowerets are tender.

In a small bowl, mix egg yolk with cream, stirring until blended. Add to soup. Bring soup just to boiling point, stirring constantly. Serve in small bowls. Sprinkle with parsley.

Makes 6 servings.

Soup is a favorite beginning to a Czechoslovakian meal. It is usually served with tasty additions like the cauliflower.

VEGETARIAN CHILI

Senator Bill Nelson, FLORIDA

2½ cups kidney beans
1 teaspoon salt
1 cup tomato juice
1 cup raw bulgur
4 cloves garlic, crushed
1½ cups onion, chopped
3 tablespoons olive oil
1 cup carrots, chopped
1 cup celery, chopped
2 teaspoons ground cumin
1 teaspoon basil
1 teaspoon chili powder
2 cups tomatoes, chopped
½ lemon, juiced
3 tablespoons tomato paste
3 tablespoons dry red wine
¼ cup cheddar cheese, grated
2 teaspoons parsley, chopped
Dash of cayenne pepper
Salt and pepper to taste

Soak kidney beans for 3 to 4 hours in enough water to cover. Add more water and salt. Cook until tender, about 1 hour.

Heat tomato juice to a boil. Pour over bulgur. Cover and let stand at least 15 minutes. Sauté garlic and onions in olive oil. Add carrots, celery, spices, and seasonings (except cayenne pepper).

When vegetables are almost cooked, add cayenne pepper. Combine beans and vegetable mixture with tomatoes, lemon juice, tomato paste, and wine.

Cover and heat in 350 degree oven. Garnish with cheese and parsley.

Makes 6 to 8 servings.

SENATOR LINCOLN'S
WHITE CHILI

Senator Blanche Lincoln, ARKANSAS

1	medium onion, chopped
2	garlic cloves, minced
1	tablespoon olive oil
½	cup green chilies, chopped
2	teaspoons ground cumin
1½	teaspoons oregano
¼	teaspoon ground cloves
2¼	teaspoons cayenne pepper
8	cups great northern beans, canned
6	cups chicken broth
6 to 8	boneless chicken breasts
3	cups Monterey Jack cheese, grated
	Sour cream
	Salsa

Sauté onions and garlic in oil in a large skillet. Add green chilies and seasonings. Add undrained beans and chicken broth.

Chop chicken breasts into cubes. Add chicken to skillet mixture and cook for 20 to 30 minutes. Add 1 cup of Monterey Jack cheese and stir until melted.

Serve in bowls with remaining grated Monterey Jack cheese, sour cream, and salsa as toppings.

Makes 8 servings.

FAMOUS SENATE RESTAURANT BEAN SOUP

★

Senator Jack Reed, RHODE ISLAND

> 2 pounds small navy beans
> 4 quarts water
> 1½ pounds ham hocks
> 1 onion, chopped
> 2 tablespoons butter
> Salt and pepper to taste

Wash navy beans and run through hot water until beans are white again. Place beans in a large pot with water and ham hocks. Boil slowly for 3 hours, covered.

Braise the onion in butter until light brown. Add to bean soup. Season with salt and pepper, and then serve. Do not add salt until you are ready to serve.

Makes 8 servings.

Whatever uncertainties may exist in the Senate of the United States, one thing is sure: bean soup is on the menu of the Senate Restaurant every day.

The origin of the culinary decree has been lost, but there are several oft-repeated legends.

One story has it that Senator Fred Thomas Dubois of Idaho, who served in the Senate from 1901 to 1907 and was chairman of the committee that supervised the Senate Restaurant, gaveled through a resolution requiring that bean soup be on the menu every day.

Another account attributes the bean soup mandate to Senator Knute Nelson of Minnesota, who expressed his fondness for it in 1903.

In any case, senators and their guests are always assured of a hearty, nourishing dish. They know they can rely on its delightful flavor and epicurean qualities.

SANTA FE SOUP

Representative Spencer Bachus, ALABAMA

  2 pounds ground turkey or beef
  1 onion, chopped
  1 ranch-style dressing mix
  2 packages taco seasoning mix
 16 ounces (1 can) black beans, undrained
 16 ounces (1 can) kidney beans, undrained
 16 ounces (1 can) pinto beans, undrained
 16 ounces (1 can) diced tomatoes with chilies, undrained
 16 ounces (1 can) tomato wedges, undrained
 32 ounces (2 cans) white corn, undrained
  2 cups water
     Sour cream
     Cheddar cheese, shredded
     Green onions, chopped

Cook meat and onion together until meat is browned. Stir ranch-style dressing mix and taco seasoning mix into meat. Add beans, tomatoes, and corn with juices from all. Add water. Simmer for 2 hours. If mixture is too thick, add more water as needed.

Garnish each serving with sour cream, shredded cheese, and green onions.

Serve with tortilla chips.

Makes 4 quarts.

BURGOO

★

Senator Mitch McConnell, KENTUCKY

1	4- to 5-pound hen
6	onions, finely chopped
1	pound beef stew meat
2	green peppers, finely chopped
1	pound veal stew meat
1	medium turnip, finely diced
4	large beef or knuckle bones
8 to 10	tomatoes, peeled and chopped
¼	cup each celery, carrot, onion, parsley
2	cups shelled fresh butter beans
10	ounces (1 can) tomato puree
2	cups celery, thinly sliced
4	quarts water
2	cups cabbage, finely chopped
1	red pepper pod
2	cups fresh okra, sliced
¼	cup salt
1	tablespoon lemon juice
1	tablespoon Worcestershire sauce
1	tablespoon sugar
2	cups fresh corn (6 ears)
1½	teaspoons coarse black pepper
½	unpeeled lemon, seeded
½	teaspoon cayenne

If you make this in 2 parts, on successive days, it is not such a chore.

DAY 1

Put the first 7 ingredients in a roaster; bring to a boil and simmer slowly, covered, for about 4 hours. Let cool and strain.

Cut chicken and meat finely, removing all skin, bone, and gristle. Kitchen scissors are good for this job. Return to stock and refrigerate.

DAY 2

Lift off half of the fat, add all the vegetables except for corn , and cook another hour until thick.

Cut corn twice, scraping cobs to get the milk. Add this along with the lemon and additional seasonings. Finishing the cooking in the oven will eliminate stirring and watching. Cook, uncovered, at 300 degrees for about 2 hours until the consistency of a thick stew. This will make a gallon. If made beforehand, reheat in the oven to ensure against scorching. Serve in mugs and sprinkle with chopped fresh parsley.

Makes 10 to 12 servings.

This is best made when fresh vegetables are at their peak, but frozen vegetables and canned tomatoes can be used when necessary. This dish freezes well.

FANCY PEANUT SOUP

Senator Jay Rockefeller, WEST VIRGINIA

1½ cups peanut butter
1 quart milk
½ teaspoon salt
Freshly ground pepper
½ teaspoon vegetable seasoning
1 onion, chopped
2 celery ribs, chopped
3 tablespoons butter
3 tablespoons flour
1 quart chicken stock
½ cup peanuts, chopped

In a pan over low heat, soften the peanut butter to allow for easy mixing with the milk. Add milk, salt, pepper, and vegetable seasoning. Bring to a boil and then set aside.

Sauté the onion and the celery in butter—do not allow to brown. Stir in the flour, as if making gravy. Add the chicken stock and stir constantly until mixture comes to a boil.

It saves time and elbow grease if the stock has already been brought to a boil. Remove from heat. Combine with the peanut butter and milk mixture.

Return to the stove and, over a very low heat, cook until all ingredients are well blended. The soup may be served either cold or hot. After ladling the soup into the individual bowls, sprinkle the chopped peanuts over the top for garnish.

Makes 12 servings.

CONGRESSIONAL BEAN SOUP (CROCK POT)

★

1	pound small white beans
8	cups water
2	cups ham, diced
1	cup onion, diced
1	cup celery, chopped
2	tablespoons parsley leaves, chopped
1	teaspoon salt
¼	teaspoon black pepper
1	each bay leaf

Assemble ingredients in a crock pot.

Cover and cook on low 8 to 10 hours or until beans are tender.

Makes 8 servings.

This savory bean soup made with ham, celery, and parsley leaves is perfect served with a loaf of French bread on the side.

ITALIAN SOUP

Senator Scott Brown, MASSACHUSETTS

16-ounce	can tomatoes
8	cups of water
2	envelopes Lipton's (or other dry) chicken soup
½	package frozen mixed vegetables
½	package frozen spinach
1	large onion
⅓	cup elbow macaroni, cooked and drained
	Pinch each of chopped parsley, basil, pepper, and oregano

In a large pot mix tomatoes and water. Bring to a boil. Add soup mix. Cook 10 minutes. Add mixed vegetables, spinach, and onion. Cook until vegetables are tender. Add macaroni. Cook 10-15 minutes. Add spices and simmer 10 more minutes.

Makes about 12 servings.

CHICKEN CHOWDER

Senator Scott Brown, MASSACHUSETTS

  1 package frozen broccoli
  5 stalks of celery, chopped
  1 medium onion, chopped
  2 cups of water
10¾ ounce can of reduced fat chicken broth
  1 cup of cold skim milk
  ½ cup flour
1½ cups cooked chopped skinned chicken breast
  1 cup skim milk
  6 ounces Swiss cheese, grated

In a heavy saucepan mix broccoli, celery, onion, water, and broth. Bring to a boil. Turn down heat and simmer for 10 minutes. Shake cold milk and flour in a tightly sealed container until smooth. Gradually stir into hot mixture. Heat to boiling. Stir in chicken and the other cup of milk. Simmer over low heat, stirring occasionally until evenly heated, about 10 minutes. Stir in cheese. Serve when cheese is melted.

Makes 10 servings

Senator Brown's wife writes: "Chowders make wonderful meals but our children don't like seafood. This is a nice alternative. It's hot and filling but it's prepared with chicken instead of fish."
—Gail Huff

TOMATO SOUP

Senator Jeff Merkley, OREGON

¼	cup olive oil
1	onion, chopped
4 to 6	cloves garlic, diced
42 to 56	ounces (3 to 4 cans) diced tomatoes, no salt added *or* the equivalent of fresh tomatoes, peeled and chopped
2	carrots
2	cans (29 ounces) vegetable or chicken broth
2	bay leaves
1	tablespoon (or to taste) sugar
	Basil to taste
	Vermouth to taste (optional)
	Parmesan cheese, for garnish

Sauté chopped onion and garlic with generous amount of olive oil until soft.

Add tomatoes and chopped carrots, cover, and simmer for at least 1 hour—longer if possible.

Puree tomato and onion mixture in blender until smooth.

In a large soup pot, add the puree to the vegetable or chicken broth.

Add remaining ingredients: bay leaves, basil, sugar, and vermouth and heat on low.

Garnish with freshly grated parmesan cheese.

Makes 8 servings.

SIDE DISHES

★ 4

Vegetables, Potatoes,
Grains, and Beans

KENYAN VEGETABLE CURRY

★

President Barack Obama

2	large onions, finely chopped
2	tablespoons oil
1	teaspoon cumin seeds
1	teaspoon mustard seeds, preferably black
8	medium potatoes (scrubbed or peeled), quartered
1½	teaspoons fresh ginger, minced
1	tablespoon ground cumin
1	tablespoon whole coriander, crushed
1	chili pepper (or ½ teaspoon cayenne pepper)
½	teaspoon ground turmeric
1	teaspoon salt
½	teaspoon ground cinnamon
⅛	teaspoon ground cloves
1	large garlic clove, minced and crushed
4 to 6	ounces (1 small can) tomato paste
½	pound green beans, trimmed
1	medium eggplant, cubed
½	pound fresh green peas, shelled (or a 10-ounce package, frozen and thawed)
1	bunch leafy greens such as kale, spinach, collards, well washed then drained (or a 10-ounce package, frozen and thawed)
1½	cups cooked or canned (rinsed and drained) chickpeas
½	teaspoon salt or more, to taste
	Half of a small cauliflower, broken into florets

Heat oven to 350 degrees. Have available one 8-quart, heavy, ovenproof skillet or Dutch oven with a lid (or have aluminum foil available). If you cut recipe in half, a 6-quart pot will do.

In the skillet or Dutch oven, brown the onions in moderately hot oil along with the cumin and mustard seeds. Add the potato pieces (peeling is optional) and stir to coat each piece with the spices. Add the remaining spices and garlic and continue to stir for several minutes. Thin the tomato paste with about ⅔ cup of water and stir into the pot. Lower heat to medium. Add vegetables, one at a time, cooking for a minute or so between each addition, and put in the cooked chickpeas last.

Bake the mixture: cover with a lid or seal with foil and bake in a preheated oven for about 45 minutes, checking after the first 20 minutes. The consistency should be rather thick, but add water if necessary to prevent burning. Stir occasionally to prevent sticking. Serve over steamed rice or with Indian bread (such as naan).

Makes 6 servings.

SOUFFLÉED CORN

★

Senator Christopher Bond, MISSOURI

6	ears corn
¾	cup butter, divided
½	cup sugar, divided
1	tablespoon flour
1½	teaspoons baking powder
½	cup evaporated milk
2	eggs, well beaten
1	teaspoon cinnamon

Preheat oven to 350 degrees. Cut corn kernels from cob. Melt ½ cup butter. Stir in ¼ cup sugar. Gradually add flour and baking powder. Blend in milk and eggs, then add corn. Mix well. Pour into a greased 8" round baking dish. Bake 35 minutes or until done. Remove from oven.

Melt remaining butter and combine with remaining sugar and the cinnamon. Brush on top of soufflé while it is still hot.

Makes 6 to 8 servings.

Freshly picked corn is one of the treats of summer in Missouri.

BROCCOLI CASSEROLE

Senator Thomas Carper, DELAWARE

¼ cup onion, finely chopped
6 tablespoons butter, divided
2 tablespoons flour
½ cup water
8 ounces Cheez Whiz (or similar product)
2 packages frozen broccoli, chopped, thawed, and drained
3 eggs, well beaten
½ cup bread crumbs

In a large skillet, sauté onions in 4 tablespoons margarine. Add flour and water; cook on low heat until thick. Add Cheez Whiz and combine sauce and broccoli. Add eggs and mix gently until blended.

Place mixture in a greased 1½-quart dish, cover with crumbs, and dot with rest of margarine. Bake at 325 degrees for 30 minutes.

Makes 8 servings.

ZUCCHINI AND CHERRY TOMATOES

Senator Christopher Bond, MISSOURI

5   small zucchini
¼   cup butter
¼   cup onion, finely chopped
½   clove garlic, minced
¾   cup cherry tomatoes, halved
2   tablespoons sesame seeds, toasted
¼   cup parsley, finely chopped
    Salt and freshly ground pepper to taste

Slice zucchini on the bias into ½" slices. In a 4-quart pan of rapidly boiling water, blanch zucchini for 1 minute. Rinse with cold water, drain, and pat dry.

Melt butter, add onion and garlic, and sauté until soft and golden brown. Add zucchini, cover, and cook for 2 minutes. Add tomatoes, cover, and cook for 1 minute. Season with salt and pepper. Add sesame seed and parsley. Toss. Adjust seasonings to taste.

Makes 6 servings.

A trip to the state fair in Sedalia, Missouri, is an annual family ritual. Our son, Sam, loves the excitement of the midway, the children's barnyard, and the many agricultural and livestock displays. The giant zucchini are amazing, but the homegrown ones are fine in this tasty vegetable duo.

COLESLAW

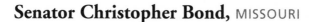

Senator Christopher Bond, MISSOURI

1   cup sour cream
¼   cup mayonnaise
3   tablespoons apple cider vinegar
4   tablespoons sugar
¼   teaspoon garlic salt
½   teaspoon salt
    Dash pepper
1   large head cabbage
5   carrots, sliced
1   red pepper, seeded
1   green pepper, seeded
1   bunch green onions
    Pepper to taste

Combine sour cream, mayonnaise, vinegar, sugar, garlic salt, salt, and pepper for dressing.

Quarter cabbage and slice thinly. Do not cut too finely.

Peel carrots and slice very thinly into rounds. Chop peppers and onions.

Pour dressing mixture over cabbage, carrots, peppers, and onions. Toss and refrigerate.

Makes 12 servings.

When Sam and I are lucky enough to find the white bass running at the Lake of the Ozarks, our fish fry includes this tangy coleslaw, plus corn on the cob and sautéed zucchini.

LEMON YAM PUFF

★

Senator Christopher Bond, MISSOURI

4   pounds sweet potatoes
1   cup brown sugar, packed
½   cup butter, softened
½   teaspoon salt
2   teaspoons orange rind, grated
2   teaspoons lemon rind, grated

Preheat oven to 350 degrees. Cook unpeeled whole sweet potatoes in boiling water for 30 minutes or until tender. Drain and reserve liquid.

Peel potatoes and mash until smooth. If mixture seems dry, add some reserved liquid. Add remaining ingredients and beat until light and fluffy.

Transfer to a greased 2-quart casserole. Bake for 30 minutes and serve hot.

Makes 8 to 10 servings.

This wintertime favorite has its origins in Ste. Genevieve County. French settlers founded the community prior to 1750. My ancestors were among the earliest to take up residence on the Missouri side of the Mississippi River. One member of the family was a member of the convention that framed the Missouri constitution.

NEW POTATOES IN BURNED BUTTER

★

Senator Mike Crapo, IDAHO

10   new potatoes, 1 to 2" in diameter
½   cup butter
     Salt and pepper to taste

Peel potatoes. Place whole potatoes in saucepan and barely cover with water. Simmer until barely tender. Melt butter in a separate pan; brown until almost ready to burn (this is very tricky).

Place drained new potatoes in a small bowl; drizzle hot butter over potatoes. Cut new potatoes into smaller pieces; season to taste with salt and pepper.

Makes 4 servings.

RICE AND MUSHROOM CASSEROLE

★

Senator Christopher Bond, MISSOURI

2 cups onion, chopped
2 cups fresh mushrooms, sliced
½ cup butter
1 cup beef consommé
1 cup water
1 cup uncooked rice
 Salt and freshly ground pepper to taste
 Snipped chives

Preheat oven to 350 degrees. Sauté onions and mushrooms in butter. Add consommé and water. Mix in rice and season with salt and pepper.

Transfer to a buttered 2-quart casserole. Bake covered for 45 minutes or until done. Garnish with snipped chives.

Makes 6 servings.

My mother is a marvelous cook and introduced my wife to this dish after we were married. It is great with chicken, game, or pork.

HASH BROWN CASSEROLE

Representative Tom Latham, IOWA

- 2 pounds frozen hash browns
- ½ cup butter
- 1 medium onion, diced
- 10½ ounces (1 can) cream of chicken soup
- 1 small carton whipping cream
- 8 ounces sour cream
- 2 cups cheddar cheese, shredded
- 2 cups Rice Krispies

Place frozen hash browns in a 9" × 13" glass dish. Melt ¼ cup butter, add diced onion, and sauté until tender. Remove from heat and let cool 5 minutes.

Add soup, whipping cream, sour cream, and shredded cheese to butter and onions. Mix well and pour over top of hash browns.

Melt remaining ¼ cup of butter, add Rice Krispies, and pour on top of hash browns.

Bake uncovered at 350 degrees for 1 hour.

Makes 8 servings.

Note: May be prepared ahead of time and refrigerated overnight.

SUMMER SQUASH CASSEROLE

Representative Steve Buyer, INDIANA

9 small yellow squash
4 eggs
1 cup sugar
¾ cup butter
⅓ medium onion, chopped
Salt and pepper to taste

Clean and cut squash into small cubes. Boil until tender. Drain and mash with potato masher. Add eggs and sugar. Mix well. Melt butter and sauté onion. Add to squash mixture. Add salt and pepper.

Place in an 8" × 8" casserole coated with nonstick spray.

Bake uncovered for 1½ hours at 350 degrees. Remove when golden brown.

Makes 8 servings.

Serve hot with crusty bread!

ARIZONA BAKED BEANS

★

Senator John McCain, ARIZONA

  1 medium onion, chopped
  1 teaspoon butter
 16 ounces (1 can) red kidney beans
 16 ounces (1 can) B&M baked beans
  1 cup ketchup
  1 cup brown sugar, packed
  1 tablespoon apple cider vinegar
  1 teaspoon mustard
  4 strips fried bacon, cooled and crumbled

In a skillet, sauté chopped onion in butter. In a large baking pot combine kidney beans, baked beans, ketchup, brown sugar, vinegar, mustard, and bacon.

After combining and stirring enough to mix the ingredients, add the sautéed onion. Mix well. Bake in a covered dish at 350 degrees for 35 minutes or until piping hot.

Makes 10 servings.

A wonderful Southwest taste treat!

KUGELIS POTATO CASSEROLE

Senator Richard J. Durbin, ILLINOIS

- 10 large red potatoes
- 1 large onion
- 5 strips bacon, diced
- ½ cup hot milk or evaporated milk
- 3 eggs, beaten
- 2 teaspoons salt
- ¼ teaspoon pepper

Peel and grate potatoes. (A food processor makes this job easy.) Grate onion. Fry diced bacon until crisp. Pour bacon fat and bacon over potatoes. Add hot milk. Add eggs one at a time, beating. Add salt and pepper and mix well.

Pour into greased 9" × 13" baking pan. Bake in preheated 400 degree oven for 15 minutes. Reduce heat to 375 degrees and bake for 45 minutes or until firm when tested by inserting a knife in center.

Makes 12 servings.

Kugelis is an authentic Lithuanian potato side dish. My mother, Ann Durbin, came to this country from Lithuania as a child. Her mother, who was the family's sole support, had to be very frugal with family finances.

My mother feasted on this delicious, yet inexpensive, dish many times while she was growing up in East St. Louis. (East St. Louis is a town in Illinois.) Although this recipe is not her mother's, she tested many kugelis recipes before finding the best one in a very old Lithuanian cookbook.

Anyone who tries this recipe will not be disappointed . . . or hungry!

CREAMY WHIPPED POTATOES

Representative William Clay, MISSOURI

 5 pounds medium potatoes
 2 teaspoons salt
 8 ounces (1 package) whipped cream cheese
   with chives
 ¼ teaspoon pepper
 1 teaspoon garlic powder
 6 tablespoons margarine or butter
 1 cup heavy or whipping cream
 ¼ cup almonds, sliced
   Paprika

About 1½ hours before serving, peel potatoes and cut into quarters. In a 5-quart saucepan over high heat, boil potatoes with 1 teaspoon of salt and enough water to cover. Reduce heat to low; cover and simmer for 20 minutes or until potatoes are tender. Drain well. Preheat oven to 375 degrees. In a large bowl, combine potatoes, cream cheese, pepper, garlic powder, 4 tablespoons margarine or butter, and 1 teaspoon salt.

With potato masher, mash until smooth. Gradually add heavy cream, mixing well after each addition. Grease 9" × 13" glass dish. Dot potatoes with 2 tablespoons margarine or butter. Sprinkle with sliced almonds and paprika. Bake for 30 minutes or until top is golden. An hour before serving, put the potatoes in the oven and heat for 30 minutes at 375 degrees.

Makes 16 servings.

SAUTÉED COLLARD GREENS WITH GARLIC AND SCALLIONS

★

Representative Charles Rangel, NEW YORK

2   teaspoons olive oil
3   cups collard greens, chopped or shredded
1   clove garlic, minced
2   scallions, minced
1   tablespoon feta cheese, crumbled

In a large nonstick skillet or a wok, heat oil over medium heat.

Add collards and garlic and sauté, stirring constantly, until collards are just wilted, about 4 or 5 minutes.

Add scallions before the collards are finished cooking.

Serve hot, topped with feta cheese.

Makes 4 servings.

Optional: Sauté a medium-sized, chopped, ripe tomato with collards and garlic.

GRANDMA'S CABERNET RISOTTO

Representative Mike Thompson, CALIFORNIA

- 3 tablespoons unsalted butter
- 1 tablespoon olive oil
- ½ yellow onion, diced
- 3 garlic cloves, crushed
- 1½ cups arborio or Carnaroli rice
- 1 cup cabernet sauvignon
- 5 to 6 cups chicken stock, hot
- ¼ cup dried tomatoes packed in oil, drained and minced
- 1 cup (4 ounces, or more to taste) Parmigiano-Reggiano, grated
  Kosher salt
  Black pepper in a mill

Heat the butter and olive oil together in a large saucepan over low heat. When the butter is melted, add the onion and garlic, and sauté until transparent, 7 to 8 minutes. Add the rice and stir with a wooden spoon until each grain begins to turn a milky white, about 2 minutes. Add the wine and continue to stir until it is completely absorbed by the rice. Keeping the stock hot over low heat, add the stock, ½ cup at a time, stirring after each addition until nearly all the liquid is absorbed. Continue to add stock and stir until the rice is tender but not mushy, a total of 18 to 20 minutes. Stir in the tomatoes and cheese, taste again, and season with salt, pepper, and, if you like, more cheese.

Serve immediately.

Makes 6 servings.

Because of the long history of Italian immigration, risottos are a staple in many California home kitchens. I grew up in St. Helena,

(continued)

near the northern end of the Napa Valley. My grandparents lived nearby, and once a week during my childhood, I went to their home for dinner. Sometimes I would help my grandmother prepare my favorite dish, a red wine risotto flavored with sun-dried tomatoes—decades before they were trendy. I learned to make this dish by watching my grandmother cook it in a cast-iron Dutch oven; she never wrote down a formal recipe. She used a ladle to add stock, not a measuring cup, and she judged when the risotto was done by how it tasted. My advice on how to achieve the perfect consistency is, simply, "practice makes perfect." I strongly recommend that the red wine be cabernet sauvignon, but you can substitute a good zinfandel, if you insist.

SPINACH SOUFFLÉ

Senator Jeanne Shaheen, NEW HAMPSHIRE

1   pound fresh spinach or Swiss chard
¼   cup butter or margarine
¼   cup all-purpose flour
1¼ teaspoon salt
¼   teaspoon pepper
1   cup milk
1   teaspoon instant minced onion
1   teaspoon salt
⅛   teaspoon nutmeg
3   eggs, separated
¼   teaspoon cream of tartar

Prepare and cook spinach or Swiss chard; chop and drain thoroughly. Heat oven to 350 degrees.

Butter a 1-quart dish or casserole. Melt butter in saucepan over low heat. Blend in flour, ¼ teaspoon salt, and pepper. Cook over low heat, stirring, until mixture is smooth and bubbly. Remove from heat and then stir in milk. Heat to boiling, stirring constantly. Boil and stir 1 minute. Remove from heat. Stir in onion, 1 teaspoon salt, and nutmeg.

In a large mixer bowl, beat egg white and cream of tartar until stiff; set aside. In a small mixer bowl, beat egg yolk until very thick and lemon colored; stir into white sauce mixture. Stir in spinach. Stir about ¼ cup of egg whites into sauce mixture and gently fold into remaining egg whites.

Carefully pour into casserole dish. Set casserole into pan of water (1" deep). Bake 50 to 60 minutes or until puffed and golden and until a silver knife inserted halfway between the edge and center comes out clean. Serve immediately.

Makes 4 to 6 servings.

SWEET POTATOES

Senator Thomas Carper, DELAWARE

<table>
<tr><td>2</td><td>pounds sweet potatoes</td></tr>
<tr><td>16</td><td>ounces (1 can) whole-berry cranberry sauce</td></tr>
<tr><td>½</td><td>teaspoon cinnamon</td></tr>
<tr><td>⅔</td><td>cup self-rising flour</td></tr>
<tr><td>⅔</td><td>cup brown sugar, firmly packed</td></tr>
<tr><td>⅔</td><td>cup quick cooking oats, uncooked</td></tr>
<tr><td>¼</td><td>cup plus 2 tablespoons margarine or butter</td></tr>
<tr><td>1</td><td>cup miniature marshmallows</td></tr>
</table>

Cook potatoes in enough boiling water to cover for 20 minutes or until tender. Let cool to touch. Peel and mash potatoes. Stir in whole cranberry sauce and cinnamon.

Spoon into a lightly greased 2-quart casserole. Combine flour, sugar, and oats. Cut in margarine or butter until mixture resembles coarse crumbs.

Spoon over sweet potatoes. Bake at 375 degrees for 20 minutes. Top with marshmallows and bake until golden brown.

Makes 8 servings.

HOPPIN' JOHN

★

Senator Mitch McConnell, KENTUCKY

2 cups fresh or frozen black-eyed peas
¼ pound of bacon
2 small red pepper pods
2 cups uncooked regular rice
Salt

Cover peas with water. Simmer peas, bacon, and peppers in a covered pot over low heat for 1½ hours or until tender.

Add rice, cover, and cook over low heat, stirring frequently until rice is cooked. Add more water during cooking if necessary. Add salt to desired taste.

Makes 8 servings.

IDAHO POTATO LOLLIPOPS

Senator James Risch, IDAHO

POTATO LOLLIPOPS

- 6 medium Idaho russet potatoes (70 count), peeled
- Oil for deep-frying
- 2 tablespoons chives, minced
- Salt and fresh-cracked black pepper to taste
- 18 lollipop sticks
- Minced chives

BACON-MUSTARD AÏOLI

- 2 egg yolks
- Juice and zest of 1 lemon
- 1 clove garlic
- 1 cup canola oil
- ½ cup olive oil
- 4 strips bacon, cooked crisp, crumbled
- 2 tablespoons stone-ground mustard
- 2 tablespoons chives, thinly sliced
- Salt and fresh-cracked black pepper to taste

CHEDDAR BÉCHAMEL

- 3 tablespoons unsalted butter
- 2 tablespoons all-purpose flour
- 1 cup low-fat (2%) milk, plus more as needed for reheating
- 2 cups cheddar cheese, finely grated
- Salt and fresh-cracked black pepper to taste

ARUGULA CREAM

- ½ tablespoon unsalted butter
- 1 medium yellow onion, diced

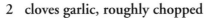

2   cloves garlic, roughly chopped

2   cups firmly packed fresh arugula, washed, dried

     Zest of 1 lemon

½   cup heavy cream

     Salt and fresh-cracked black pepper to taste

POTATOES

Using center section of each potato, slice 3 horizontal 1"-thick slices (trim off ends of potatoes). Using a small, round cookie cutter, cut 3 circles (or use other cutter for desired shape). Reserve ends for other use. Soak cut potatoes briefly in cool water to prevent them from discoloring.

Place potatoes in pot of heavily salted water; bring to simmer. Cook until potatoes begin to soften, 5 to 8 minutes; remove from water and dry at room temperature. Potatoes should be cooked ½ to ¾ of the way through.

BACON-MUSTARD AÏOLI

In food processor, pulse yolks, lemon juice, zest, and garlic until incorporated and smooth, about 1 minute. Combine oils; slowly add to egg mixture with processor running so mixture emulsifies. If mixture gets too thick, add 1 to 2 tablespoons milk or water. Transfer to small bowl. Using rubber spatula, fold in bacon, mustard, and chives. Season to taste with salt and pepper. Set aside in refrigerator for up to 2 days.

CHEDDAR BÉCHAMEL

Melt butter in small, heavy saucepan over medium heat. Stir in flour; cook to a smooth paste, about 1 minute. Whisk in milk; cook until

(continued)

mixture is thick and smooth, 2 minutes. Reduce heat to low. Add cheese, salt, and pepper; stir until cheese has melted, 2 minutes. Remove from heat; adjust seasoning. Reserve warm.

ARUGULA CREAM

In a heavy saucepan, melt butter over medium-high heat. As butter begins to brown, add onion and garlic; cook until onion becomes translucent, 2 to 3 minutes. Add arugula, lemon zest, cream, salt, and pepper. When cream reaches a simmer, lower heat; cook until liquid is reduced by half, 7 to 8 minutes, watching closely so cream does not boil over. Remove from heat; transfer to blender or food processor. Puree until smooth. Adjust seasoning. Reserve warm.

ASSEMBLY

Liberally season potatoes with salt and pepper. Heat oil in deep-fryer to between 350 and 360 degrees, and finish cooking potatoes for 6 to 8 minutes until fork tender and golden brown. Remove potatoes; carefully slide lollipop stick into each for service.

For each portion, spoon 1 tablespoon each of aïoli, béchamel, and arugula cream onto a plate. Carefully place potato lollipop so it stands secured in sauces. Garnish with minced chives. Serve at once.

Makes 6 small-plate servings.

Quote from Mrs. (Vicki) Risch
We like this recipe because it features the world's best potato, the Idaho potato, and because it is fun to serve. Put 1 or 2 potato lollipops on a small serving plate with a spoonful of each of the three dips and let the tasting begin. Everyone will have a different opinion on which dip is best.

MAIN DISHES

★ 5

Casseroles, Soufflés,
Savory Pies, and
Sandwiches

MICHELLE OBAMA'S MACARONI AND CHEESE

President Barack Obama

- 1 pound elbow macaroni
- 3 tablespoons butter
- 1 cup Swiss cheese, shredded
- 1 cup Parmesan cheese plus 2 tablespoons for topping, grated
- 2 cups sharp cheddar cheese, grated
- ⅞ teaspoon (or to taste) salt
- 1 cup heavy cream
- 1 egg
- ¼ cup milk

Preheat oven to 350 degrees. Butter a 9" × 13" pan or casserole dish and set aside.

In a large pot of boiling water, cook pasta until tender, 5 to 8 minutes.

Drain pasta in a colander and then return to pot while still hot. Dot with cut-up pieces of butter.

Slowly sprinkle the cheeses (reserving 2 tablespoons of the Parmesan) and salt onto the hot pasta, turning noodles with a wooden spoon to spread cheese evenly. Stir gently so as not to break up noodles. Set aside.

Pour heavy cream into a microwave-safe measuring cup or bowl and microwave until warm, about 30 seconds. Add egg and milk to cream and whisk with a fork.

Stir the cream mixture into the pasta. Pour the mixture into the baking dish. Spread evenly and sprinkle the top with the remaining 2 tablespoons of parmesan.

Bake until cooked through and cheese is lightly browned on top, about 20 minutes.

Serve warm.

Makes 6 to 8 servings.

HAM MOUSSE

Senator Christopher Bond, MISSOURI

4 cups ground cooked ham
1 large onion, diced
½ cup golden raisins
2 to 3 tablespoons dry sherry
1 teaspoon prepared horseradish
½ teaspoon nutmeg
2 teaspoons Dijon mustard
2 tablespoons unflavored gelatin
2 tablespoons cold water
1 cup chicken stock
1 cup heavy cream, whipped
2 tablespoons parsley, finely chopped

Combine ham, onion, and raisins in a food processor. Puree, or put through the finest blade of a meat grinder 3 times. Combine meat mixture, sherry, horseradish, nutmeg, and mustard. Set aside.

Soften gelatin in cold water for 5 minutes. Bring chicken stock to a boil, add gelatin, and stir over medium heat until dissolved. Add to ham mixture; blanch thoroughly. Cool 10 to 15 minutes. Fold whipped cream and parsley into mixture.

Turn into a well-oiled 5-cup mold. Chill 3 hours or until firm. Unmold on a plate garnished with sweet gherkins or stuffed green olives. Serve with very thin slices of French or rye bread.

Makes 16 to 20 servings.

Note: Because of its richness, serve the mousse in small portions when using as an entrée.

During a Fourth of July trip to Hannibal, Missouri, for the annual Tom Sawyer Days, we were treated to this deliciously simple ham mousse served with a spicy homemade mustard. The events highlighted are the Tom Sawyer and Becky Thatcher look-alike contest and the fence-painting contest on the banks of the Mississippi River.

CHEESE SOUFFLÉ

★
Senator Charles Grassley, IOWA

8 slices day-old bread, crusts trimmed
8 slices Old English cheese
6 eggs, well beaten
3 cups milk
½ teaspoon salt
½ teaspoon dry mustard
2 cups diced ham or cooked chicken (optional)

Lay bread in bottom of buttered 9" × 13" pan. Top with cheese. Mix eggs, milk, salt, and dry mustard. Pour well-beaten egg mixture over top.

Note: If you use meat, put it under the cheese.

Cover and refrigerate overnight. Before baking, top with crushed cornflakes mixed with melted butter.

Bake for 1 hour at 350 degrees. Serve while hot.

Makes 10 servings.

From Nan, whose husband is in the navy.

TAILGATE HERO SANDWICH

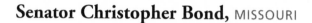

Senator Christopher Bond, MISSOURI

1 loaf French bread, crusty
½ cup Italian dressing
½ cup mayonnaise
 Durkee's hot sauce to taste
⅓ pound smoked turkey
⅓ pound corned beef
⅓ pound ham
⅓ pound baby Swiss cheese, thinly sliced
⅓ pound provolone, thinly sliced
⅓ pound New York cheddar cheese, thinly sliced
2 medium tomatoes, thinly sliced and drained
2 medium green peppers, thinly sliced into rings
1 red onion, thinly sliced into rings

Cut bread loaf in half lengthwise. Scoop out centers, leaving a ½" shell. Spread both halves with Italian dressing. Generously spread mayonnaise over one half and Durkee's sauce over the other.

Layer turkey, corned beef, and ham on both halves together. Layer cheeses on meats, then tomatoes, green peppers, and onion on cheeses. Carefully put halves together. Wrap sandwich tightly with foil and refrigerate. To serve, cut in 2" slices. The sandwich may be prepared and refrigerated for up to 48 hours before serving.

Makes 12 to 16 servings.

Mizzou football has always been a family affair for the Bonds. This colossal sandwich that serves a crowd is our standby for Tiger tailgates. My dad, Art Bond, who rarely missed a home game, was captain of the 1924 team that won the Missouri Valley Championship, defeating Big Ten winner Chicago.

CHICKEN CASSEROLE

★

Senator Roger Wicker, MISSISSIPPI

20 ounces (2 packages) frozen broccoli, chopped
1 package (6 ounces) Uncle Ben's wild rice mix
6 whole chicken breasts, broiled
10½ ounces (1 can) cream of mushroom soup
10½ ounces (1 can) cream of chicken soup
1 cup mayonnaise
¾ teaspoon curry powder
1 tablespoon lemon juice
1 cup sharp cheese, grated

Cook and season broccoli and wild rice according to directions. Cut chicken in large bite-sized pieces. Arrange broccoli around edge with wild rice in center. Put chicken on top.

Mix remaining ingredients (except cheese) together and pour over top. Sprinkle cheese on top.

Bake at 350 degrees for 40 minutes. Freezes well.

Makes 6 servings.

This recipe was given to us when we got married. It is great for a Sunday lunch or any time company is coming.

GARLIC ROASTED CHICKEN AND NEW BABY ROSE POTATOES AND SHALLOTS

★

Representative Loretta Sanchez, CALIFORNIA

CHICKEN

½	cup extra virgin olive oil
1	tablespoon dried rosemary
1	teaspoon dried thyme
4	whole chicken legs and thighs, unsplit
4 to 6	cloves fresh garlic, thinly sliced
	Salt and pepper to taste

NEW BABY ROSE POTATOES AND SHALLOTS

10 to 12	new baby rose potatoes, quartered
6 to 8	large shallots
3	tablespoons extra virgin olive oil
1	teaspoon caraway seeds
	Salt and pepper to taste

CHICKEN

Preheat oven to 450 degrees. In a small bowl, mix together olive oil, rosemary, and thyme. Place unsplit chicken legs into a baking dish and generously brush both sides with the olive oil mixture to marinate. Sprinkle thin slices of garlic over chicken, and salt and pepper to taste.

NEW BABY ROSE POTATOES AND SHALLOTS

Cut potatoes into quarters and peel shallots. Combine potatoes and shallots in small baking dish. Add olive oil and stir together to coat thoroughly. Sprinkle caraway seeds over potatoes. Salt and pepper to taste.

Bake chicken and potatoes for 1 hour, occasionally stirring potatoes.

Makes 4 servings.

CHICKEN SPECTACULAR

Representative Kevin Brady, TEXAS

- 1 box (6 ounces) Uncle Ben's Original Recipe Long Grain and Wild Rice
- 8 ounces (1 can) French-cut green beans
- 1 pound cooked chicken, chopped
- 1 onion, chopped
- 10½ ounces (1 can) cream of celery soup
- 10½ ounces (1 can) cream of mushroom soup
- 1 cup mayonnaise
- 1 can water chestnuts, chopped
- 2 tablespoons sugar
  Salt and pepper to taste
- 1 small jar pimentos (optional)

Prepare rice. Combine all ingredients and cook in large casserole dish at 350 degrees for 30 minutes.

Makes 4 to 6 servings.

My mother has been making this for years and it is one of my all-time favorites, one of those that challenges the depths of self-discipline.

—Cathy Brady

KING RANCH CHICKEN

Representative Pete Sessions, TEXAS

    4   boneless chicken breasts
10½   ounces (1 can) cream of chicken soup
   14   ounces (1 can) Rotel diced tomatoes and peppers
    2   cups cheddar cheese, shredded and halved
    1   bag tortilla chips

Cook chicken breasts—boil, bake, microwave, or BBQ them. Cut the cooked chicken into small squares.

Mix cream of chicken soup and Rotel, including juice. Add 1 cup shredded cheddar cheese. Mix in tortilla chips.

Pour the entire mixture into a 2-quart buttered casserole. Cover with the remaining cheese. Cover with plastic wrap and microwave for 6 minutes. If you do not have a microwave, cover with foil and bake at 300 degrees for 30 minutes.

Makes 4 servings.

SENATOR LANDRIEU'S OVEN JAMBALAYA

★

Senator Mary Landrieu, LOUISIANA

2 cups Uncle Ben's converted rice
2 pounds chicken, cut up
1 pound sausage, cut up
1 cup French onion soup
1 cup beef broth
8 ounces tomato soup
½ cup green onion, chopped
½ cup green pepper, chopped
4 bay leaves
1 teaspoon parsley
8 ounces butter, cut into slices
Pepper to taste

Mix all ingredients (except butter) in a baking dish. Place pats of butter on top. Bake at 350 degrees for 30 minutes.
Makes 6 servings.

Simple and satisfying!

TETRAZZINI

Representative Sue Myrick, NORTH CAROLINA

1   pound rotini pasta
1   tablespoon margarine or butter
½   cup Parmesan cheese, divided and grated
4   boneless chicken breasts
2   tablespoons margarine or butter
2   cups chicken broth
⅔   cup flour
4   cups half-and-half
¼   cup sauterne
1   teaspoon salt
1   cup mushrooms (optional)

Cook rotini according to directions and drain. Toss with margarine and Parmesan cheese.

Cook chicken, saving broth. Cut chicken into small pieces.

To cook sauce, melt 2 tablespoons of margarine. Mix in chicken broth while adding the flour to thicken. Next add half-and-half. Cook until it thickens and bubbles. Add the sauterne and salt and let simmer.

Layer pasta, chicken, mushrooms, and sauce in a casserole dish. Cover with ¼ cup Parmesan cheese. Bake at 350 degrees for 25 to 30 minutes.

Makes 4 servings.

FRITTATA

★────────────────────────────────────

Senator Patrick Leahy, VERMONT

¼ cup olive oil
3 medium onions, thinly sliced
1 cup Italian plum tomatoes, drained and coarsely
   chopped
6 eggs, beaten
¼ cup Parmesan cheese, grated
½ teaspoon salt
   Freshly ground pepper to taste
2 tablespoons parsley, chopped
2 tablespoons dried basil
2 tablespoons butter

Heat oil in skillet. Add onions and cook over moderate heat until lightly brown. Add tomatoes and turn up heat. Cook, stirring for 5 minutes. Cool.

Combine eggs with cheese, salt, pepper, parsley, and basil. Add drained onion and tomato mixture. Wipe out skillet with paper towel.

Add butter to skillet and heat to foaming, but do not brown. Add egg mixture. Turn heat to very low and cook for 15 minutes or until only bottom is firm.

Place under heated broiler for 30 minutes to set the top. Do not brown. Cut in wedges and serve from pan.

Makes 4 servings.

FAVORITE CHEESE ENCHILADAS

★

Senator Tim Johnson, SOUTH DAKOTA

    8   corn tortillas

SAUCE
   ½   cup onion, chopped
   4   cloves garlic, crushed
   3   tablespoons olive oil
   2   ounces green chili, diced
   1   pound tomatoes (fresh or canned), cooked, peeled, and chopped
   1   cup tomato juice
   ¼   teaspoon powdered oregano
   ¼   teaspoon basil
   1   cup strong vegetable or beef broth
 1½   tablespoons cornstarch
   ¼   cup water

FILLING
  10   ounces sharp cheddar or Monterey Jack cheese
2 or 3   scallions, chopped
   ¼   cup parsley, chopped
   ½   cup mushrooms, chopped
   ¼   cup black olives, sliced

Sauté onion and garlic in olive oil until onion is transparent. Add chili, tomatoes, tomato juice, and herbs. Simmer 5 minutes. Add broth. Dissolve cornstarch in water and stir into sauce. Cook slowly 10 minutes. If sauce is too thick, add a little water.

(continued)

Place a corn tortilla gently on heated sauce. Remove tortilla when it starts to warm. Arrange some filling ingredients on the saucy side. Roll it up and place in oiled oblong baking dish.

Repeat with remaining tortillas. Pour remaining sauce over rolled-up tortillas. Bake at 350 degrees for 15 to 20 minutes.

Makes 4 servings.

Fantastic flavor.

ANN'S CHICKEN POT PIE

★

Representative Jim Turner, TEXAS

11	ounces Swanson's canned white meat chicken, drained
15	ounces succotash, drained
10½	ounces (1 can) cream of mushroom soup
1	package frozen deep-dish pie shells (2 shells)
	Pepper to taste

Preheat oven to 375 degrees. In a large bowl, mix chicken, succotash, soup, and pepper. Pour into first pie shell.

While second pie shell is still in its tin, trim away only the crimped edge with a knife. Remove the shell from its tin and center it, upright, on top of pie. Let stand a couple of minutes for crusts to soften; crimp edges together. Cut an *X* into the top of the pie shell to vent.

Put on a cookie sheet and bake at 375 degrees for 5 minutes; reduce heat to 350 degrees and bake about 20 minutes more or until crust is lightly browned.

Makes 12 to 16 servings.

From Ann Gray, who is the director of Jim's Orange, Texas, office. She says this is a lifesaver for her. . . . She's always in a hurry and has a hungry teenager at home! She adds a salad in a bag, and the meal is done!

SUNDAY BRUNCH CASSEROLE

Senator Jay Rockefeller, WEST VIRGINIA

    4   cups day-old bread, cubed
    2   cups cheddar cheese, grated
   10   eggs, lightly beaten
    4   cups milk
    1   teaspoon dry mustard
    1   teaspoon salt
   ¼   teaspoon onion powder
        Dash of pepper
8 to 10 strips cooked bacon, crumbled
   ½   cup cooked or canned mushrooms, sliced
   ½   cup tomatoes, peeled and chopped

Place bread in bottom of a greased 2-quart casserole. Sprinkle with cheese. Beat eggs, milk, mustard, salt, onion powder, and pepper together. Pour over cheese and bread.

Sprinkle with bacon, mushrooms, and tomatoes. Refrigerate, covered, up to 24 hours.

Bake, uncovered, in preheated 325 degree oven for 1 hour or until set.

Makes 8 servings.

Recipe from Carolanne Griffith, in *Mountain Measures: A Second Serving* (Charleston, WV: Junior League of Charleston, 1984), a collection of West Virginia recipes.

EASY BUT RICH
BEEF CASSEROLE

★

Representative John Dingell, MICHIGAN

1½ pounds stewing beef, trimmed and cut into
    2" pieces
½ cup red dinner wine
10½ ounces (1 can) undiluted beef consommé
4 ounces (1 can) mushrooms, drained
    Salt and pepper to taste
1 medium onion, peeled and sliced
¼ cup bread crumbs
¼ cup flour

Combine beef, wine, consommé, mushrooms, salt, pepper, and onion in casserole dish. Mix bread crumbs with flour and stir into mixture.

Cover and bake in preheated 300 degree oven for about 3 hours or until beef is tender.

Makes 6 servings.

SENATOR'S MIDNIGHT SUPPER

Senator Richard Lugar, INDIANA

2 slices toast

3 eggs

2 tablespoons sour cream or imitation sour cream

Salt to taste

1 tablespoon butter

1 cup asparagus spears

5 ounces cheddar cheese soup (undiluted)

Paprika, for garnish

Trim crusts from toast. Lightly beat together eggs, sour cream, and salt with a fork. Then melt butter in skillet and scramble egg mixture. In separate pan, heat asparagus spears.

In third pan, heat cheese soup. Place hot, drained asparagus spears on toast. Top with scrambled eggs. Pour cheese soup over top of eggs.

Serve with sausage, bacon, or Canadian bacon and a green salad.

Makes 2 servings.

> This is the sort of thing Dick likes when he gets home late at night from meetings or speaking engagements. I can put it together in a hurry, and most of the ingredients are always on hand on the pantry shelf. The dish is also good for brunch.
>
> —Char Lugar

EXTRA MEATY LASAGNA

★

Senator Kent Conrad, NORTH DAKOTA

1½ pounds extra-lean ground beef
1 medium onion, chopped
1 pound sweet Italian sausage links
16 ounces (1 can) seasoned meaty tomato sauce
1 teaspoon oregano
1 teaspoon pepper
1 teaspoon garlic powder
3 quarts water
Dash of salt
¼ cup vegetable or olive oil
8 ounces lasagna noodles
3 cups low-fat creamed cottage cheese
2 tablespoons dried parsley flakes
1 egg, beaten
1 pound mozzarella cheese, shredded
1 cup Parmesan cheese, grated

Brown ground beef and onion. Add a small amount of oil to moisten, if necessary. Remove ground beef and onion. Retain fat in pan and add sausage links. Brown on all sides. In saucepan place tomato sauce, oregano, pepper, and garlic powder. Add ground beef and onion, mixing well. Simmer. Drain fat from sausage, pat with towel to remove excess oil and fat. Place sausage in saucepan with tomato sauce and meat mixture. Continue simmering. *Do not boil.* Stir often.

Bring water, salt, and oil to boil in large pot. Add noodles, one at a time. Bring to a second boil, then follow cooking directions on package. While noodles are cooking, mix cottage cheese, parsley,

(continued)

and beaten egg in a bowl. Set aside. Remove sausage from sauce and cut into ¼" round slices. Stir sauce to avoid sticking. After sauce has cooked for 15 minutes (or when sausage is cooked thoroughly), remove from heat.

Drain noodles. Layer one half of the noodles in a lightly greased 9" × 13" baking dish spread with half of the cottage cheese mixture. Add half of the sausage slices, then half of the sauce and meat mixture; sprinkle half of the shredded or sliced mozzarella cheese. Repeat layers. Sprinkle Parmesan cheese on top. Bake for 30 to 35 minutes at 375 degrees.

Makes 10 servings.

Note: This recipe can be prepared in advance and refrigerated prior to baking. Bake for 45 minutes to 1 hour. Wait a few minutes after baking, then slice and serve.

This is a great entrée just for the family or for dinner guests. The only other dish you need with it is a tossed salad to make a complete meal. We use prepared tomato sauce because it's so good and saves time.

BEEF STROGANOFF

Senator Robert Byrd, WEST VIRGINIA

1½ pounds round steak
¼ cup butter
1 cup mushrooms, sliced
1 clove garlic, minced
½ cup onion, chopped
1¼ cups tomato soup
1 cup sour cream
  Salt and pepper to taste

Cut beef into long thin strips. Brown beef in butter in a heavy skillet. Add mushrooms, garlic, and onion. Cook until lightly browned.

Blend in tomato soup, sour cream, salt, and pepper. Cover and simmer about 1 hour or until beef is tender. Stir occasionally. Serve with hot cooked rice.

Makes 6 servings.

DUCK AND WILD RICE CASSEROLE

Representative Marion Berry, ARKANSAS

           2 medium ducks (3 cups meat)
           3 stalks celery
           1 onion, halved
        1½ teaspoons salt
          ¼ teaspoon pepper
           6 ounces wild rice
           6 ounces long-grain rice
          ½ cup butter or margarine
          ½ cup onion, chopped
          ¼ cup flour
           4 ounces (1 can) mushrooms, sliced,
               with juice reserved
        1½ cups half-and-half
           1 tablespoon parsley
        1½ teaspoons salt
          ¼ teaspoon pepper
               Slivered almonds

Boil ducks for 1 hour in water with celery, onion halves, salt, and pepper. Remove meat and cube. Reserve broth. Cook rice according to package directions. Melt margarine, sauté onions, and stir in flour. Drain mushrooms, reserving broth. Add mushrooms to the onion mixture. Add enough duck broth to the mushroom broth to make 1 ½ cups of liquid. Stir this into the onion mixture. Add half-and-half, parsley, salt, and pepper.

Place in greased 2-quart casserole dish. Sprinkle almonds on top. Bake covered at 350 degrees for 15 to 20 minutes. Uncover and bake for 5 to 10 minutes more. Chicken substituted for duck also makes a tasty dish.

Makes 6 to 8 servings.

ISLAND SAMOAN CHOP SUEY

Representative Eni Faleomavaega, SAMOA

1½ bundles bean-thread long rice noodles
1 pound meat (beef, pork, or chicken)
   Garlic powder to taste
   Pepper to taste
5 tablespoons olive oil
½ cup onion, chopped
2 or 3 garlic cloves, chopped
3 ounces gingerroot, chopped
12 ounces chicken or beef broth
3 cups mixed fresh or canned vegetables
   (chopped carrots, celery, green peppers, cabbage)
¼ cup Kikkoman Shoyu sauce
3 tablespoons sesame oil

Soak the strings of long rice in a bowl of hot water to soften. Season the meat, chopped into stir-fry size, with garlic powder and pepper in a bowl. Pour the oil in an 8-quart pot and add onions and garlic; heat until onions sizzle. Add meat. Stir and turn the meat until cooked; add the chopped gingerroot at the same time. Keep the mixture moist by adding broth to the pot.

Add the chopped vegetables. Drain the water from the bowl of long rice noodles and chop the strings into 4" lengths.

Add the Shoyu sauce and sesame oil and mix it all together. At the same time, add more broth to balance the juices and contents.

The heat should be medium high and reduced later to medium.

Makes 6 servings.

Good luck and enjoy!

GIOVANNI'S POLLO MARINATO

Representative Elton Gallegly, CALIFORNIA

1	pound chicken breasts, boneless and skinned
6	ounces white wine
6	ounces olive oil
1	lemon, juiced
1	teaspoon salt
12	ounces penne pasta
3	cups whipping cream
3	ounces porcini mushrooms
3	ounces sundried tomatoes
1	teaspoon fresh basil
½	teaspoon tarragon
½	teaspoon dill
	Salt and pepper to taste
½	cup Parmesan cheese, grated

Marinate chicken breasts in wine, olive oil, lemon juice, and salt for 2 hours. Boil water for pasta and cook approximately 15 minutes. Slice chicken into thin strips and cook on low heat. Add in the whipping cream.

When chicken appears almost done, add mushrooms, sundried tomatoes, and spices. Toss with penne pasta and serve with grated Parmesan cheese on top.

Makes 4 servings.

This recipe is compliments of our favorite restaurant, Pastabilities.

ADAM AND EVE'S CHILI

Representative Adam Schiff, CALIFORNIA

3 pounds ground beef or turkey
2 tablespoons olive oil
1 medium onion, chopped
30 ounces tomato sauce
12 ounces tomato paste
15 ounces stewed tomatoes
½ teaspoon pepper
½ teaspoon oregano
½ teaspoon cumin
2 teaspoons garlic salt
2 teaspoons cayenne (1 teaspoon for mild)
½ teaspoon Tabasco pepper sauce
1 teaspoon soy sauce
2 teaspoons Worcestershire sauce
6 ounces beer
3 16-ounce cans pinto beans

Brown ground beef or turkey in 2 tablespoons oil. Drain liquid.

Chop onion and add tomato sauce, tomato paste, stewed tomatoes, pepper, oregano, cumin, garlic salt, cayenne, Tabasco sauce, soy sauce, and Worcestershire sauce.

Simmer, covered, and cook for ½ hour. Add beer and pinto beans. Simmer 1 hour or longer.

Makes 6 to 8 servings.

PALACHINKE (FILLED PANCAKES)

★

Senator George Voinovich, OHIO

PANCAKES

    1¼   cups of cake flour

    1¼   teaspoon baking powder

    ½   teaspoon salt

    1   teaspoon sugar

    1   cup milk

    2   egg yolks, beaten

    2   tablespoons butter, melted

    2   egg whites, stiffly beaten

FILLING

    1   pound creamed cottage cheese

    2   eggs

    ¼   cup sugar (can be less)

PANCAKES

Sift flour, add baking powder, salt, and sugar; sift once more. Add milk to egg yolks. Add flour mixture gradually; mix to smooth batter. Add butter. Fold in egg whites. Bake on hot greased griddle.

FILLING

Mix all ingredients well. Spread on each pancake, roll up, and place side by side in greased cake pan.

Bake 30 minutes at 350 degrees.

Makes 6 servings.

> This is another of my wife Janet's recipes that I have enjoyed.

CHILI CON CARNE WITH TOMATOES

★

Senator Jeanne Shaheen, NEW HAMPSHIRE

1	pound ground beef
2	medium onions, chopped (about 1 cup)
1	cup green pepper, chopped
1	pound fresh or 12 ounces canned tomatoes
8	ounces (1 can) tomato sauce
2	teaspoons chili powder
1	teaspoon salt
⅛	teaspoon cayenne pepper
⅛	teaspoon paprika
15½	ounces (1 can) kidney beans, drained

Cook and stir ground beef, onion, and green peppers in large skillet until meat is brown and onion is tender. Drain off fat.

Stir in remaining ingredients except kidney beans. Heat to boiling. Reduce heat. Cover and simmer 2 hours, stirring occasionally (or cook uncovered for 45 minutes).

Stir in beans. Heat thoroughly.

Makes 6 servings.

HUSHWEE
MEDITERRANEAN DISH

★

Representative Nick Rahall, WEST VIRGINIA

1½ cups long-grain rice
½ pound coarsely ground lamb
¼ cup pine nuts
4 tablespoons butter
1 teaspoon salt
¼ teaspoon pepper
1 teaspoon cinnamon
¼ teaspoon allspice
3 cups chicken broth

Soak rice in warm water for 15 minutes, then drain. Brown lamb and pine nuts in butter.

Stir spices in with the meat-and-nut mixture. Add drained rice and stir until the nuts, meat, and spices are thoroughly mixed.

Stir in chicken broth and bring to a boil. Reduce heat, cover, and simmer for 15 minutes or until the liquid is absorbed. Serve with a side dish.

Makes 4 servings.

MICA'S PASTA AND CHICKEN

Representative John Mica, FLORIDA

2   pounds boneless, skinless chicken breast, diced
⅜   cup olive oil, divided
3   tablespoons black pepper
3   tablespoons garlic salt
5   tablespoons dried or fresh basil
¼   cup olive oil
8   cloves garlic, peeled and chopped
2   32-ounce cans plum tomatoes, peeled
¼   cup sugar
2   tablespoons oregano
1   pound linguini pasta
1   cup Romano cheese, grated

In a large frying pan, sauté cut-up chicken breast in ⅛ cup olive oil; cover chicken with pepper and garlic salt and sprinkle lightly with basil. Only cook slightly.

In separate large pot add ¼ cup of olive oil; heat, but do not burn oil, adding 8 chopped garlic cloves. Lightly sauté garlic but do not brown. Add plum tomatoes slowly, which should fry lightly in the oil and garlic (crush plum tomatoes before adding).

Add the rest of the pepper, garlic salt, and basil and the sugar and oregano; cook for 30 minutes, adding water if mixture becomes too thick. Then add partially cooked chicken and cook for 30 to 40 minutes. Boil water and cook pasta. Serve sauce over pasta and mix in grated Romano cheese.

Makes 8 servings.

Enjoy!

BREAKFAST "BRAINS AND EGGS"

Representative Howard Coble, NORTH CAROLINA

2½ tablespoons bacon grease

5 ounces (1 can) pork brains in gravy
(Rose brand preferred)

¼ teaspoon salt

¼ teaspoon freshly ground black pepper

4 eggs

⅓ cup whole milk

Melt bacon grease in an iron skillet on low heat. Add pork brains to heated grease. Stir with a fork. Add salt and pepper and stir.

Whisk eggs and milk together. Increase heat and add egg mixture to brains. Scramble to desired consistency.

Serve immediately over toast. For a truly southern dish, serve with grits and apple butter.

Makes 2 servings.

When I was a youngster, my mom used to prepare brains 'n' eggs for breakfast. It was a fairly regular breakfast, not at all unusual. So that's when I started eating them. I've enjoyed them ever since, but I can't find any on Capitol Hill. I'll admit the name of the dish is not the most appetizing, but try 'em! You might like 'em!

BEEF STROGANOFF

Senator Mike Johanns, NEBRASKA

BEEF

1 pound beef sirloin
1 tablespoon flour
½ teaspoon salt
2 tablespoons butter or margarine
½ cup onion, chopped
1 clove garlic, minced
3 ounces (1 can) mushrooms, drained

GRAVY

2 tablespoons butter
3 tablespoons flour
1 tablespoon tomato paste
1 10-ounce can condensed beef broth
2 tablespoons dry white wine
1 cup sour cream

This is my favorite recipe because I love beef and the way my wife, Stephanie, prepares the dish.

BEEF

Trim and cut beef into strips. Mix flour and salt and lightly bread the beef. Melt butter over medium heat and add floured beef, onion, and garlic and cook until lightly browned. Add mushrooms.

GRAVY

Add butter to pan of meat. Mix flour and tomato paste in separately to avoid lumps and then add the beef broth to create the "gravy." Add the combined mixture to the beef pan and add wine.

Cook on medium low until beef is tender—the longer it cooks, the more tender it will be. If the mixture gets too thick, add water or more wine, depending on your preference (I generously add wine!). Add sour cream at the end but with enough time for it to warm to temp.

Serve over boiled noodles.

Makes 4 servings.

MEATS

★ 6

Beef, Pork, Ham,
and Game

PORK CHOPS WITH APPLE

Senator George Voinovich, OHIO

8 loin pork chops
  Salt and pepper to taste
½ cup apple juice or cider
3 tablespoons ketchup
½ cup soy sauce
½ cup brown sugar
2 tablespoons cornstarch
½ teaspoon ground ginger
2 apples (we like Golden Delicious)

Bake chops with salt and pepper in roasting pan, uncovered, for 30 minutes at 350 degrees. Turn chops over midway during cooking.

Combine juice, ketchup, soy sauce, brown sugar, cornstarch, and ginger. Cook over medium heat until thickened. Spoon some juice from the roasting pan into the sauce to thin.

Core apples; cut into rings and place one ring on each chop. Pour sauce over pork chops. Bake 30 minutes longer. Baste several times.

Makes 8 servings.

I like this with rice and broccoli.

PORK PIE

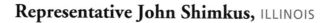

Representative John Shimkus, ILLINOIS

1	pound bulk pork sausage
1	cup cooked ham, cubed
½	teaspoon ground sage
½	teaspoon pepper
1	cup green pepper, chopped
½	cup onion, chopped
½	cup celery, chopped
10½	ounces (1 can) cream of chicken soup
1	apple, sliced
¼	cup Parmesan cheese, grated
1	pie crust
	Butter or margarine

Cook and stir sausage in 10" skillet until done. Drain. Stir in ham, sage, pepper, green pepper, onion, celery, and cream of chicken soup.

Place in ungreased deep-dish pie plate or quiche pan. Place sliced apple on top and sprinkle with cheese.

Cover with pie crust and seal. Prick pie crust and dot with butter or margarine. Bake at 375 degrees for 30 to 40 minutes.

Makes 8 servings.

Enjoy!

FAVORITE MEAT LOAF

Senator Thad Cochran, MISSISSIPPI

1½ pounds ground beef

1 cup cracker crumbs

2 eggs, beaten

8 ounces (1 can) tomato sauce, with tomato bits

½ cup onion, finely chopped

2 tablespoons green pepper, chopped

1 medium-sized bay leaf, crushed

1 teaspoon thyme leaves, dried

1 teaspoon marjoram leaves, dried

Preheat oven to 350 degrees. Mix ingredients thoroughly.
Place in lightly greased loaf pan. Bake for 1 hour.
Makes 8 servings.

FAVORITE CABBAGE ROLLS

Senator Robert Byrd, WEST VIRGINIA

          1   pound lean ground beef
          1   cup cooked white rice
          1   small onion, chopped
          1   teaspoon salt
        ¼   teaspoon pepper
          1   egg
        10   cabbage leaves
          1   tablespoon vegetable oil
        16   ounces (1 can) tomato sauce
        ¼   cup water

Mix ground beef, cooked rice, chopped onion, salt, pepper, and egg together. Trim off thickest part of stem from cabbage leaves.

Divide meat into equal portions, wrap each in a leaf, and fasten with wooden picks.

Brown cabbage rolls slightly in oil. Add tomato sauce and water to pan. Cover and cook slowly for about 40 minutes.

Makes 5 servings.

MOOSE SWISS STEAK

★

Representative Don Young, ALASKA

    3   pounds moose steak
    2   tablespoons lemon juice
    ¼   cup flour
    1   teaspoon dry mustard
    1½   teaspoons salt
    ¼   teaspoon pepper
    ⅓   cup shortening
    1   small onion, sliced
    14½ ounces canned tomatoes

Sprinkle meat with lemon juice and pierce with fork to tenderize. Mix dry ingredients together and add meat to mixture.

Brown meat slowly in shortening. Place in a 2-quart casserole dish and cover with sliced onions and tomatoes.

Bake at 325 degrees for 1½ to 2 hours.

Makes 6 servings.

An Alaskan favorite!

MANDARIN PORK STEAKS

Senator Christopher Bond, MISSOURI

1	cube beef bouillon
1/3	cup hot water
1	teaspoon ground ginger
2	teaspoons salt
1	tablespoon sugar
1/4	cup honey
1/4	cup soy sauce
4 to 6	pork arm or blade steaks

Place bouillon and water in a large glass, stainless steel, or enamelware pan. Stir until dissolved. Add all ingredients except pork. Mix well. Add pork.

Refrigerate at least 2 hours, preferably overnight, turning occasionally.

Preheat oven to 350 degrees or prepare outdoor grill. Remove pork steaks from marinade and place on rack in shallow roasting pan.

Bake for 50 minutes or until done, or grill 4" from coals 12 to 15 minutes on each side or until juices run clear. Baste each side frequently with marinade.

Makes 4 to 6 servings.

TERIYAKI BEEF

★

Senator Tim Johnson, SOUTH DAKOTA

1¼ cups brown sugar
1 cup soy sauce
½ teaspoon ginger, grated
½ garlic clove, crushed
⅛ teaspoon sesame oil
2 or 3 pounds flank steak or 4 small ¾" thick steaks

Combine sugar, soy sauce, ginger, garlic, and oil, stirring well.
Pour over steak and marinate 3 hours, turning meat occasionally.
Broil or barbecue to taste.
Makes 4 servings.

NEBRASKA BEEF BRISKET

★

Senator Benjamin Nelson, NEBRASKA

1   Nebraska beef brisket
2   teaspoons liquid smoke
1   large onion, sliced
    Salt and pepper to taste

Rub a good cut of Nebraska beef brisket with your favorite spices. Add liquid smoke, sliced onions, salt, and pepper.

Wrap tightly in foil and place in a shallow 9" × 13" baking pan.

Bake at 250 degrees for 6 hours.

Let sit for 10 minutes before slicing or shredding.

Makes 4 to 6 servings.

PRIME RIB

★

Senator Benjamin Nelson, NEBRASKA

5 pounds Nebraska prime rib roast, boned
2 teaspoons Kitchen Bouquet
   Salt and pepper to taste
   Whole garlic cloves

Rub roast with Kitchen Bouquet, salt, and pepper. Arrange in shallow baking pan with whole garlic cloves and more Kitchen Bouquet.

Bake covered at 425 degrees for 1 hour. Turn oven down to 200 degrees. Cook for another 1 to 1½ hours. Meat thermometer should read 130 degrees.

Let sit for 10 minutes before carving. Serve with creamy horseradish sauce or mushroom sauce.

Makes 12 servings.

PORK ROAST IN MUSTARD SAUCE

Senator Jon Kyl, ARIZONA

1 4-pound boneless pork loin
½ teaspoon salt
¼ teaspoon pepper
¼ teaspoon garlic powder
⅓ cup Dijon mustard
⅓ cup apple cider vinegar
Pepper to taste
2 cups cream
2 tablespoons Dijon mustard
2 tablespoons cold butter
Freshly ground pepper
Salt to taste

Trim excess fat from roast. Sprinkle roast with salt, pepper, and garlic powder. Spread ⅓ cup mustard over roast and place in large Dutch oven. Cover and bake for 3 hours at 325 degrees or until meat thermometer reads 170 degrees. Remove roast and set aside to keep warm. Add vinegar and freshly ground pepper to pan. Boil mixture, scraping bottom of pan.

Cook mixture until it is reduced in volume by half. Stir in cream; simmer for 5 minutes. Remove from heat; stir in 2 tablespoons mustard, butter, and salt to taste. Spoon half of hot sauce over sliced pork roast and serve with remaining sauce.

Makes 12 to 14 servings.

Note: I usually prepare half of this recipe when serving my family. It is very easy and very tender, and leftovers reheat well. It takes 3½ hours to prepare and is not suitable for freezing.

IOWA CHOPS

Senator Tom Harkin, IOWA

2   Iowa pork chops

STUFFING
- ½   cup whole-kernel corn
- ½   cup bread crumbs
- ¾   tablespoon parsley
- ½   tablespoon onion, chopped
- ½   cup apple, diced
- 1   tablespoon whole milk
  Pinch of sage
  Pinch of salt
  Pinch of pepper

BASTING SAUCE
- ¼   cup mustard
- ¼   cup honey
- ½   teaspoon salt
- ¼   teaspoon rosemary
  Pinch of pepper

Cut pocket into side of chops. Combine stuffing ingredients and stuff chops. Brown in pan, then bake at 350 degrees for about 1 hour. Baste often with basting sauce mixture.

Makes 2 servings.

BEEF STROGANOFF

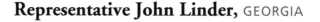

Representative John Linder, GEORGIA

2 pounds sirloin steak, cubed
¼ pound butter
1 onion, minced
1 green pepper, diced
1 tablespoon Worcestershire sauce
1 tablespoon garlic powder
1 cup mushrooms, sliced
2 tablespoons red wine vinegar
1 pint sour cream
1 cup heavy cream
  Dash of Tabasco sauce
  Salt and pepper to taste

Cook steak cubes in butter. Add onion and green pepper; cook until soft. Add remaining ingredients.
Makes 4 servings.

GRAPE DOGS

★

Representative Steven LaTourette, OHIO

2 bottles of Heinz chili sauce
8 ounces grape jelly
2 packages of hot dogs, sliced into ¾" to 1" pieces.
   Mini, bite-sized hot dogs can also be used.

Heat chili sauce in a medium saucepan until boiling. Blend in the jelly and stir in 2 packages of your favorite hot dogs, sliced.
Simmer on low heat for 20 minutes. Serve warm on toothpicks. Grape dogs can also be prepared in a crock pot.
   Makes 10 servings

I used this "Grape Dogs" recipe several years ago at a "Real Men Can Cook" contest for a charity in Lake County, Ohio, and won. Grape Dogs are a crowd-pleasing appetizer at tailgate and cocktail parties; also, the tangy sauce is delicious with meatballs.

BACON FRIED PHEASANT

Senator John Thune, SOUTH DAKOTA

1	pound bacon
2 to 3	pheasants or 4 to 6 breasts
	Garlic to taste
1	small onion
4	ounces (1 can) mushrooms, sliced and drained
1	can water chestnuts, drained
	Pinch of pepper
6	rosemary pieces
¼	teaspoon parsley flakes
1	teaspoon salt
4	stalks of celery, sliced
1½	cups water
2	ounces dry white cooking wine or apple cider

Fry bacon. Remove and fry cut-up pheasant in fat from bacon. Add garlic to taste, 1 small onion, mushrooms, and water chestnuts. Add a pinch of pepper, 6 rosemary pieces, ¼ teaspoon parsley flakes, and 1 teaspoon salt. Simmer 5 minutes.

Take out pieces as they brown. Place in casserole on bed of celery pieces. Combine water and dry white cooking wine or apple cider.

Add vegetables from browning to casserole. Bake at 300 degrees for 3 hours.

Crumble bacon and add to casserole when 1 hour is remaining. Also baste pheasant at that time.

Makes 4 to 6 servings.

BABY BACK RIBS

Senator John McCain, ARIZONA

        4   racks of baby back ribs
    ¼   cup ground pepper
    ¼   cup salt
    ¼   cup garlic powder
        4   lemons, quartered

Mix together pepper, salt, and garlic power and coat ribs evenly and marinate overnight.

Place ribs on a barbeque at 400 degrees.

Squeeze fresh lemon evenly over ribs every few minutes while cooking.

Makes 8 to 10 servings.

POULTRY AND SEAFOOD

★ 7

Chicken, Duck,
Shellfish, and Fish

DOVE ON THE GRILL

Senator Richard Shelby, ALABAMA

Dove (allow at least 2 per person)
Salt and pepper to taste
Worcestershire sauce to taste
Bacon (1 slice per bird)

Sprinkle dove with salt, pepper, and Worcestershire sauce. Wrap each dove with bacon. Secure with toothpick if necessary.

Cook over a medium fire until done, about 20 to 30 minutes. Turn occasionally.

Variation: Wrap ½ strip of bacon around a water chestnut and a boneless dove breast. Season lemon butter with Worcestershire sauce and baste frequently.

Cook on grill or broil until bacon is done.

KOREAN CHICKEN

★

Senator Daniel Akaka, HAWAII

CHICKEN

    5   pounds chicken

    1   tablespoon salt

    1   cup flour

    2   tablespoons vegetable oil

SAUCE

    1   scallion, chopped

    1   small red pepper, chopped

    1   clove garlic, chopped

    6   tablespoons sugar

    ½   cup soy sauce

    1   teaspoon sesame oil

Cut chicken in bite-sized pieces and sprinkle with salt. Let chicken stand overnight in refrigerator. Roll chicken in flour and fry in oil. After frying, mix sauce ingredients. Dip chicken in sauce and serve. Makes 16 servings.

SAXBY'S QUAIL

★

Senator Saxby Chambliss, GEORGIA

- 10 quail
  - Salt and pepper
- 16 ounces butter
- 1 tablespoon flour
- 2 tablespoons Worcestershire sauce
- 2 tablespoons lemon juice
- 2 cups water
- 1 cup fresh mushrooms, sliced

Salt and pepper the quail. Melt the butter and add the flour, Worcestershire sauce, lemon juice, and water. Bring to a boil.

Pour this mixture over the birds and add mushrooms. Bake in a covered baking dish for 2 hours at 350 degrees. This is wonderful with grits. Not suitable for freezing.

Makes 10 servings.

I hope that others will enjoy this!

POPPY SEED CHICKEN

Senator Roger Wicker, MISSISSIPPI

6 boneless, skinless chicken breasts
10½ ounces (1 can) cream of mushroom soup
4 ounces sour cream
4 ounces margarine
1 cup Ritz crackers, crushed
1 tablespoon poppy seeds

Cook chicken and chop into bite-size pieces. Place in buttered 9" × 13" casserole dish. Mix soup and sour cream. Spread over chicken.

Melt margarine. Mix with crushed crackers. Add poppy seeds and spread on top of casserole. Bake for 30 minutes at 30 degrees. Serve over rice.

Makes 6 servings.

MEXICANA CHICKEN

★

Senator Christopher Bond, MISSOURI

10¾ ounces (1 can) cream of chicken soup

10¾ ounces (1 can) cream of celery soup

10½ ounces (1 can) chicken broth

4 ounces (1 can) green chili

12 corn tortillas, broken into small pieces

3 cups cooked chicken, chopped

8 ounces cheddar cheese, chopped

Combine soups, broth, chili, and tortillas. Let stand 30 minutes.

Preheat oven to 350 degrees. Place half of the mixture in a greased 9" × 13" baking dish. Cover with chicken.

Pour remaining mixture over chicken and sprinkle with cheese. Bake uncovered for 25 minutes.

Makes 8 to 10 servings.

SUPER FISH

Senator Charles Grassley, IOWA

3 pounds frozen haddock or cod fillets
Salt to taste
2 to 3 tablespoons onion, minced
2 tablespoons butter
1 cup sour cream
10½ ounces (1 can) cream of mushroom soup
10½ ounces (1 can) cream of celery soup
1 tablespoon parsley

Thaw fish and place in 8" × 12" baking dish, still in block size. Sprinkle with salt. Sauté onion in butter.

Mix all other ingredients except parsley and heat together. Pour over fish and bake for 30 to 40 minutes at 375 degrees or until fish is done. Sprinkle with parsley before baking or put fresh parsley on top a few minutes before baking is finished.

Makes 6 to 8 servings.

This is another of my mother's creations. She cooks it in the microwave these days!

CHICKEN BREASTS IN PAPRIKA CREAM SAUCE

Senator Harry Reid, NEVADA

- ½ cup onion, finely chopped
- ½ cup butter
- 1 tablespoon paprika
- 4 skinless chicken breasts, deboned
- ¼ cup white wine
- ¼ cup chicken stock
- 1 cup heavy cream
  Salt and pepper to taste
- 1 teaspoon lemon juice

Boil onion 3 to 4 minutes. Drain well. Melt butter in casserole dish over low heat. Then add onions, but do not brown. Add paprika and remove from heat. Roll chicken breasts in mixture and bake covered at 350 degrees until chicken breasts are done. Remove from oven and set aside.

Heat sauce mixture of wine and chicken stock. Bring to a boil and let cook for 3 to 4 minutes. Remove from heat. Add cream and stir well. Cook over low heat for 2 to 3 minutes. Add salt, pepper, and lemon juice to taste. Pour this mixture over baked chicken breasts. Serve with garnish.

Makes 4 servings.

Tasty and delicious with potatoes or rice!

IMPERIAL CRAB

Senator Barbara Mikulski, MARYLAND

1   pound back-fin crabmeat
Dash of salt
Cayenne pepper
1   green pepper, diced
2   eggs, well beaten (set aside 2 tablespoons)
5   tablespoons mayonnaise, divided
1   tablespoon onion, chopped

Pick over crabmeat. Combine with salt, cayenne pepper, green pepper, beaten eggs, 4 tablespoons mayonnaise, and chopped onion.

Fill 6 decorative serving shells with crabmeat mixture.

Add 1 tablespoon mayonnaise to remaining egg and put over each filled shell. Dot with cayenne pepper.

Bake at 350 degrees for about 30 minutes.

Makes 6 servings.

HONEY MUSTARD CHICKEN

Senator Frank R. Lautenberg, NEW JERSEY

4 to 6   chicken breasts, skinless and boneless
½   cup butter or margarine, melted
½   cup honey
¼   cup Dijon mustard
Salt and pepper to taste

Preheat oven to 350 degrees. Mix together butter or margarine, honey, mustard, salt, and pepper. Pour over chicken pieces.

Bake uncovered for approximately 45 minutes or until done, basting often.

Serve with rice or couscous.

Makes 4 to 6 servings.

SESAME CHICKEN

★

Senator John Ensign, NEVADA

2	pounds chicken breasts or chicken tenders
1	egg
2	tablespoons flour
2	tablespoons cornstarch
2	tablespoons water
1	teaspoon salt
2	teaspoons vegetable oil
¼	teaspoon baking soda
¼	teaspoon white pepper
½	cup water
¼	cup cornstarch
1	cup sugar
1	cup chicken broth
¾	cup rice vinegar
2	teaspoons soy sauce
2	teaspoons chili paste
1	teaspoon vegetable oil
1	clove garlic, finely chopped
	Oil for frying
2	tablespoons sesame seeds, toasted
	Fruit added to sauce (optional)

Cut chicken into 2½" strips. Mix next 8 ingredients and stir chicken into mixture. Cover and refrigerate 20 minutes. Mix water and cornstarch and set aside. Heat next 7 ingredients and cook to boiling. Stir in the cornstarch mixture. Cook and stir until thickened.

Remove from heat, but keep warm. Heat 1½" of oil to 350 degrees. Fry chicken, adding one at a time for 3 minutes or until light

(continued)

brown. Remove chicken with a slotted spoon and drain on paper towels.

Place chicken on heated platter. Heat sauce to boiling and pour over chicken. Sprinkle with sesame seeds. Serve with white rice.

Makes 6 servings.

This is so yummy, and my kids love it!

PACIFIC SALMON

Representative Norm Dicks, WASHINGTON

Pacific salmon, smoked
Crackers
Capers
Cream cheese
Chopped onion

Catch Pacific salmon.

Have salmon smoked and vacuum-packed in individual serving sizes.

Salmon may be frozen up to 6 months.

Serve salmon sliced with crackers, capers, cream cheese, and chopped onions.

GOVERNOR'S FISH IN COCONUT MILK

Representative Madeleine Z. Bordallo, GUAM

- 2 pounds fish (skipjack, mullet, dolphin, or island fish), sliced about 2" thick
- ½ onion, sliced
- ¼ cup apple cider vinegar
- ½ cup water
- 1 clove garlic, mashed
- 1 green pepper, sliced
- Salt and pepper to taste
- 1½ cups thick coconut milk

Put all ingredients except coconut milk in a pot and cook for about 20 minutes on medium heat or until the fish is cooked.

Add coconut milk. Remove from direct heat. Do not boil coconut milk.

Serve hot with steamed rice.

Makes 8 servings.

KADON MANOK (CHICKEN STEW)

Representative Madeleine Z. Bordallo, GUAM

½ medium onion, chopped
2 tablespoons cooking oil
1 chicken, cut up
    Salt and pepper to taste
8 medium Chinese cabbage leaves,
    cut into 1½" pieces

In a 3-quart saucepan, sauté onion in oil. Add chicken, and salt and pepper to taste. Cover pan and reduce to medium heat.

Sauté chicken until most of the juice is gone. Then add enough water to cover the chicken and cook until done.

Add Chinese cabbage to boiling broth and cook about 5 minutes.

Serve hot over rice.

Makes 4 servings.

GREAT BARBECUED KENAI SALMON

Senator Lisa Murkowski, ALASKA

½ cup apple cider
6 tablespoons soy sauce
2 tablespoons butter
1 large garlic clove, crushed
2 salmon fillets, each 2⅓ to 3 pounds
   or 1 4- to 5-pound salmon steak cut 1" thick

Prepare a marinade by combining cider and soy sauce. Bring to a boil and reduce heat. Simmer 3 minutes. Add butter and garlic and continue cooking.

Simmer, stirring occasionally, until liquid reduces and thickens enough to coat back of a spoon, about 20 minutes. Cool.

Brush marinade over salmon fillets and place skin side down on rack. Let stand 30 minutes at room temperature.

Cook on hot coals; make an aluminum foil tent over fish. Bake for 15 to 20 minutes, until fish is tender and flaky.

Makes 4 servings.

There is nothing better than fresh Alaskan salmon!

SAN FRANCISCO
SEASONED SHRIMP

Senator Dianne Feinstein, CALIFORNIA

2   tablespoons lemon juice
    Salt and black pepper to taste
3   tablespoons olive oil
1   pound of large shrimp
1   lemon, cut in wedges
1   onion, sliced in rings
3   tablespoons pimento (in a jar)
¼   cup olives, sliced

Mix lemon juice, salt, pepper, and olive oil together. Set aside. Cook and shell shrimp.

Add the shrimp to the lemon juice mixture to marinate. Let sit for at least 2 to 3 hours (overnight is even better).

Place shrimp in bowl. Garnish with lemon slices. Serve with onion, pimento, and olives.

Makes 4 servings.

SHRIMP SCAMPI

★

Representative Elton Gallegly, CALIFORNIA

1	stick butter
1	large onion, diced
4	cloves garlic
½	teaspoon garlic salt
½	teaspoon salt
½	teaspoon pepper
1	teaspoon Cavender's All Purpose Greek Seasoning
1	teaspoon parsley
1	teaspoon Worcestershire sauce
1	tablespoon fresh lemon juice
1½	pounds large peeled and deveined raw shrimp

Sauté onion in butter and then add remaining ingredients.
Simmer for approximately 7 minutes or until shrimp are done.
Best when served over long-grain brown rice.
Makes 4 servings.

JAPANESE CHICKEN SALAD

Representative Mike Honda, CALIFORNIA

CHICKEN

1 head cabbage

2 ounces (1 package) slivered almonds

3 teaspoons sesame seeds, toasted

5 green onions, diced

1 package Top Ramen noodles (chicken flavor)

½ cup cooked chicken, diced

DRESSING

¼ cup olive oil

3 tablespoons red wine vinegar

1 tablespoon sugar

1 envelope of Top Ramen seasoning (chicken flavor)

Mix cabbage, almonds, sesame seeds, and green onions. Crush Top Ramen noodles and add to cabbage mixture. Prepare dressing. Add chicken and dressing and toss. Makes 4 servings.

GRILLED TURKEY BREAST IN PITA POCKETS

Senator Richard Lugar, INDIANA

1½ pounds turkey breast tenderloins

2 limes, juiced

1 tablespoon paprika

½ teaspoon onion salt

½ teaspoon garlic salt

½ teaspoon cayenne pepper

¼ teaspoon white pepper

½ teaspoon fennel seeds

½ teaspoon thyme

10 pitas, cut in half

1½ cups lettuce, shredded

1½ cups avocado salsa (see recipe below)

1½ cups sour cream sauce (see recipe below)

Rub turkey breast with juice of limes. In a small bowl, combine paprika, onion salt, garlic salt, cayenne pepper, white pepper, fennel seeds, and thyme. Sprinkle mixture over turkey. Cover and refrigerate for at least 1 hour.

Preheat charcoal grill for direct-heat cooking. Grill turkey 15 to 20 minutes until meat thermometer reaches 170 degrees and turkey is no longer pink in the center.

Turn turkey tenderloins over halfway through grilling time. Allow turkey to stand 10 minutes. Slice in ¼" strips.

Fill each pita half with turkey, lettuce, avocado salsa, and, if desired, the sour cream sauce.

Makes 10 servings.

This recipe is one of my family favorites, a light meal of turkey pita pockets with avocado salsa and sour cream sauce.

AVOCADO SALSA

★

Senator Richard Lugar, INDIANA

- 1 avocado, diced
- 1 lime, juiced
- 2 tomatoes, seeded and diced
- ½ cup green onion, minced
- ½ cup green pepper, minced
- ½ cup fresh cilantro

In small bowl, combine avocado and lime juice.
Stir in tomatoes, green onion, green pepper, and cilantro.
Cover and refrigerate until ready to use.
Makes 3 cups.

Enjoy!

SOUR CREAM SAUCE

★

Senator Richard Lugar, INDIANA

        1   cup sour cream
        1   teaspoon salt
        ¼   cup green onion, minced
        ¼   cup green chilies, minced
        ¼   teaspoon cayenne pepper
        ½   teaspoon black pepper

In a small bowl, combine sour cream, salt, onion, chilies, cayenne pepper, and black pepper.

Cover and refrigerate until ready to use.

Makes 2 cups.

FAVORITE CRAB CAKES

Senator Barbara Mikulski, MARYLAND

1   egg
3   slices white bread
1   tablespoon mayonnaise (light)
1   tablespoon Dijon mustard
2   teaspoons Old Bay or Wye River seasoning
1   tablespoon snipped parsley (optional)
1   pound jumbo lump or back-fin crab meat
1   tablespoon vegetable oil (for frying or sautéing)
     Tartar sauce, mustard, or cocktail sauce

Beat the egg in a bowl. Remove the crusts from the bread and break the slices into small pieces. Add to the egg. Mix in the mayonnaise, Dijon mustard, Old Bay or Wye River seasoning, and parsley and beat well.

Place the crabmeat in a bowl and pour the egg mixture over the top. Gently toss or fold the ingredients together, taking care not to break up the lumps of crabmeat. Form the cakes by hand or with an ice cream scoop into 8 mounded rounds about 3" in diameter and ¾" thick. Do not pack the mixture too firmly. The cakes should be as loose as possible yet still hold their shape. Place the cakes on a tray or platter covered with wax paper, cover, and refrigerate for at least 1 hour before cooking.

Frying the crab cakes: Pour oil into a heavy skillet to a depth of about 1½". Heat the oil and fry the crab cakes, a few at a time, until they are a golden brown, about 4 minutes on each side. Remove with a slotted utensil and place on paper towels to drain.

Broiling the crab cakes: Slip cakes under a preheated broiler until nicely browned, turning to cook evenly, about 4 to 5 minutes on each side.

(continued)

Sautéing the crab cakes: Heat a small amount of clarified butter or olive oil, or a combination, in a skillet and sauté the cakes, turning several times, until golden brown, about 8 minutes total cooking time.

Makes 6 servings.

KENTUCKY HOT BROWN

Senator Mitch McConnell, KENTUCKY

¼ cup butter
6 tablespoons flour
3 cups warm milk
6 tablespoons Parmesan cheese, grated
1 egg, beaten
1 ounce cream, whipped (optional)
  Salt and white pepper to taste
8 to 12 slices toast, trimmed
  Slices of roast turkey
  Extra Parmesan cheese, grated, for topping
8 to 12 strips bacon, fried

Melt the butter and add enough flour to make a reasonably thick roux, enough so to absorb all of the butter.

Add milk and Parmesan. Add egg to thicken sauce but do not boil. Remove from heat. Fold in whipped cream. Add salt and pepper.

For each serving, place 2 slices toast on a metal or flame-proof dish. Cover the toast with a liberal amount of turkey. Pour a generous amount of sauce over the turkey and toast. Sprinkle with additional Parmesan.

Place entire dish under a broiler until the sauce is speckled brown and bubbly. Remove from broiler, cross 2 pieces of bacon on top, and serve immediately.

Makes 4 to 6 servings.

BREADS

★ 8

Yeast Breads, Quick Breads, Pancakes, and Muffins

VIRGINIA BROWN BREAD

Representative Rick Boucher, VIRGINIA

1 cup brown sugar, packed
1 cup dark molasses
3 packages active dry yeast
2 tablespoons salt
2 cups nonfat dry milk powder
7 cups very warm water
5 tablespoons butter or margarine, melted
3 eggs, lightly beaten
9 cups whole wheat flour
Approximately 8 cups white flour

Mix together all ingredients except white flour and let stand for 15 minutes. Work in enough white flour to make elastic, slightly sticky dough. Knead for several minutes.

Cover and let rise until double in bulk. Punch down dough and let rise again. Shape into 5 loaves and let rise in greased loaf pans until more than double.

Bake in preheated 350 degree oven until done, about 40 minutes. Makes 5 loaves.

Southwest Virginia brown bread is a traditional favorite in the Fightin' Ninth Congressional District of Virginia!

MARY'S SPOON BREAD

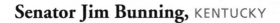

Senator Jim Bunning, KENTUCKY

  1   cup cornmeal

  2   cups milk, scalded

½   teaspoon salt

  1   tablespoon sugar

  1   cup margarine

  5   egg yolks, beaten

  5   egg whites, beaten until stiff

1½ tablespoons bourbon

Add cornmeal to scalded milk. Continue cooking and stirring until thick. Add salt, sugar, and margarine. Heat until margarine is melted. Add beaten egg yolks to mixture.

Fold in egg whites (beaten until stiff) and add bourbon. Bake in a 2-quart, greased casserole for 40 minutes at 350 degrees. Serve immediately.

Makes 6 to 8 servings.

CHERRY NUT BREAD

Senator Tim Johnson, SOUTH DAKOTA

BREAD

8	ounces (1 package) cream cheese
1	cup margarine
½	cup sugar
½	teaspoon vanilla
4	eggs
2¼	cups flour, divided
1½	teaspoons baking powder
¾	cup cherries
½	cup pecans, chopped

GLAZE

1½	cups powdered sugar
2	tablespoons milk

BREAD

Thoroughly blend cream cheese, margarine, sugar, and vanilla. Add eggs one at a time, mixing well after each addition. Gradually add 2 cups flour sifted with baking powder. Combine remaining flour with cherries and nuts. Fold in batter.

Grease 10" loaf or Bundt pan and pour batter into pan. Bake at 325 degrees for 1 hour and 20 minutes. Cool 5 minutes, and remove from pan.

GLAZE

Combine powdered sugar and milk, then drizzle over cake.

SUNFLOWER WHEAT BREAD

Senator Kent Conrad, NORTH DAKOTA

1½ cups whole wheat flour

1 cup white flour

½ cup quick-cooking rolled oats

½ cup brown sugar, packed

1 tablespoon orange peel, finely shredded

½ teaspoon baking powder

½ teaspoon baking soda

½ teaspoon salt

1¾ cups buttermilk

1 egg, beaten

½ cup sunflower seeds

2 tablespoons honey, for garnish

2 tablespoons sunflower kernels, for garnish

In a large bowl, combine whole wheat flour, white flour, oats, sugar, orange peel, baking powder, baking soda, and salt until well blended. Add buttermilk and egg; stir just until ingredients are moistened. Stir in sunflower seeds.

Pour into greased 9" × 5" bread pan. Bake at 350 degrees for 50 to 60 minutes or until bread tests done. If necessary, cover loaf with foil during the last 15 minutes of baking to prevent overbrowning.

Cool in pan for 10 minutes; turn out on a wire rack and allow to cool thoroughly before cutting. Brush top of loaf with honey and sprinkle with additional sunflower kernels, if desired.

Makes 1 loaf.

PEACH MUFFINS

Senator Christopher Bond, MISSOURI

2 cups unsifted flour

1 tablespoon baking powder

1 egg

¼ cup oil

1 cup milk

⅔ cup sugar

½ teaspoon salt

¼ teaspoon cinnamon

1 teaspoon lemon juice

¼ teaspoon vanilla

1 cup fresh peaches, chopped

Preheat oven to 450 degrees. Sift flour and baking powder together. Beat egg and stir in oil, milk, sugar, salt, cinnamon, lemon juice, and vanilla. Add in flour mixture and stir until blended. Do not overmix. Gently fold in peaches. Fill greased muffin cups ⅔ full. Bake for 20 minutes.

Makes 18 to 20 muffins.

Note: A cup of drained canned peaches packed in light syrup or water may be substituted.

OATMEAL PANCAKES

★

Senator Charles Grassley, IOWA

2	eggs, beaten
1½	cups buttermilk
1	cup oatmeal
1	teaspoon baking powder
1	teaspoon baking soda
½	teaspoon salt
1	teaspoon sugar
⅓	cup flour

Combine all ingredients and let sit a few minutes for oatmeal to soak up a bit of moisture.

Cook in a hot skillet as you do other pancakes.

Makes 8 pancakes.

MASSACHUSETTS CRANBERRY BREAD

★

Senator John Kerry, MASSACHUSETTS

¼ cup butter or margarine, softened
1 cup sugar
2 eggs
1 cup Massachusetts cranberries, chopped
½ cup water
½ teaspoon vanilla
1¾ cups flour
½ teaspoon baking soda
1½ teaspoons baking powder
1 teaspoon salt
½ teaspoon cinnamon
½ cup walnuts, chopped

Grease and flour a loaf pan. Cream the butter or margarine and sugar together in a large mixing bowl. Beat in the eggs with an electric mixer.

Stir in cranberries, water, and vanilla. Sift the flour, baking soda, baking powder, salt, and cinnamon together and stir in with the butter.

Add the chopped walnuts to the mixture and pour into the loaf pan.

Bake at 350 degrees for 55 minutes. Test with a toothpick for doneness.

Makes 1 loaf.

DATE AND NUT BREAD

Representative Ron Paul, TEXAS

      2 teaspoons baking soda
      1 pound dates, chopped
      1 pint boiling water
      3 tablespoons butter
   1½ cups sugar
      2 eggs, beaten
     ½ teaspoon salt
      3 cups flour
      1 cup walnuts, chopped
      1 tablespoon vanilla

Sprinkle baking soda over chopped dates. Pour in boiling water and stir. Add butter, sugar, and eggs to mixture. Add salt, flour, walnuts, and vanilla.

Pour batter into 4 greased 7½" × 3½" × 2" loaf pans.

Bake 45 minutes at 350 degrees or until toothpick comes out clean. Loaves require only 15 minutes preparation time and are suitable for freezing.

Makes 4 medium-sized loaves.

HOMEMADE BISCUITS

Representative Jerry Costello, ILLINOIS

2 cups Gold Medal self-rising flour
2 tablespoons Crisco shortening, room temperature
2 teaspoons buttermilk
3 tablespoons Crisco shortening, melted

Crumble flour and 2 tablespoons room-temperature Crisco. Add buttermilk to moisten.

Form into loose ball. Lay ball of dough on floured surface. Pat down gently with heavily floured hands. *Do not roll out.*

Cut biscuits.

Place in a greased 9" × 13" glass baking dish. Brush melted Crisco on top of biscuits.

Bake at 400 degrees for 15 to 20 minutes.

Makes 12 biscuits.

LEMON BLUEBERRY MUFFINS

Senator Barbara Boxer, CALIFORNIA

2	cups flour
⅔	cup sugar
1	teaspoon baking powder
1	teaspoon baking soda
2	cups blueberries, fresh or frozen
1	cup lemon yogurt
½	teaspoon salt
¼	cup butter or margarine, melted
1	egg, lightly beaten
1 to 2	teaspoons lemon peel, grated
1	teaspoon vanilla

Preheat oven to 400 degrees. Combine dry ingredients in a large bowl.

Stir in blueberries. In a separate bowl, blend wet ingredients, including lemon peel. Add wet to dry and stir until just combined. Do not over mix.

Fill greased muffin cups and bake for 20 to 25 minutes or until cake tester inserted in center of one muffin comes out clean. Cool on rack for 5 minutes before removing from pan; finish cooling on rack.

Makes 12 muffins.

CAKES AND
COOKIES

 9

COCONUT CAKE

★

Senator Benjamin Nelson, NEBRASKA

1   package yellow cake mix
1   can Eagle Brand sweetened condensed milk
1   15-ounce can cream of coconut
1   8-ounce carton of Cool Whip or a small carton of whipping cream
1   14-ounce package coconut

Bake cake according to package directions in a 9" × 12" pan.

When it is done, poke holes in the cake with a fork. Pour the condensed milk and cream of coconut over the cake. Let cool. Spread the whipped cream over the cake, then sprinkle with coconut flakes.

LEMON FLIP CAKE

Senator Richard Lugar, INDIANA

1 tablespoon butter
2 tablespoons flour
¾ cup sugar
2 egg yolks, beaten
¼ cup fresh lemon juice
1 cup milk
2 egg whites, stiffly beaten

Cream butter, flour, and sugar. Add beaten egg yolks, lemon juice, and milk.

Fold in stiffly beaten egg whites. Bake in an 8" ungreased dish set in a pan of water at 350 degrees for 35 minutes.

When cool, flip cake over onto a plate. Sauce (custard consistency) is now on the top.

> I usually serve this recipe for dessert after a light meal of turkey pita pockets with avocado salsa and sour cream sauce (see pages 146, 147, 148, respectively, for recipes).

GERMAN APPLE CAKE

Senator George Voinovich, OHIO

1 package German chocolate cake mix
2 cups (1 can) prepared apple pie filling
3 eggs
  Whipped cream
  Cinnamon

Blend all ingredients and beat as per package directions. Pour into greased and floured 9" × 13" pan. Bake at 350 degrees for 40 to 50 minutes (until top springs back.) Cool. Top with whipped cream and sprinkle with cinnamon.

This is one of my wife Janet's recipes that I have enjoyed throughout the years. . . . This is a quickie and is very moist.

SHENANDOAH VALLEY APPLE CAKE

Representative Bob Goodlatte, VIRGINIA

1 cup oil

2 cups sugar

2 large eggs

3 cups of flour

½ teaspoon cinnamon

½ teaspoon nutmeg

1 teaspoon baking soda

1 teaspoon salt

½ teaspoon vanilla

3 cups Virginia apples (tart), chopped

½ cup nuts, chopped

3 teaspoons sugar mixed with 1 teaspoon cinnamon
  for coating the tube/Bundt pan

Prepare the pan in advance by greasing and then shaking the sugar-cinnamon mixture until the sides and bottom are well coated.

Combine oil and sugar until well mixed. Add eggs, beating well after each is added. In a separate bowl, combine flour, cinnamon, nutmeg, baking soda, and salt. Add vanilla to the egg-sugar mixture and mix well. Slowly add the well-blended flour mixture into the oil and sugar. Add the apples and nuts.

Pour the batter into the pan and bake at 325 degrees for 1¾ hours.

This cake has been a favorite of our family. Its aroma in our kitchen signals the approach of fall. The Shenandoah Valley, Allegheny Highlands, Roanoke, and Lynchburg, which I am privileged to represent in Congress, are beautiful any time of the year, but they are especially vibrant when autumn colors our mountains. For generations, travelers have enjoyed the natural beauty, bounty, and hospitality of our area. You are cordially invited to explore and enjoy this beautiful part of Virginia.

APPLESAUCE CAKE

Representative Frank Wolf, VIRGINIA

CAKE

2½	cups flour
1½	cups sugar
¼	teaspoon baking powder
½	teaspoon baking soda
1½	teaspoons salt
¾	teaspoon cinnamon
½	teaspoon ground cloves
½	teaspoon allspice
½	cup butter or margarine
½	cup water
2	cups sweetened applesauce
2	eggs
1	cup raisins, chopped
¾	cup nuts, chopped

ICING

⅓	cup butter
1	cup brown sugar
½	cup cream or whole milk
	Confectioner's sugar

CAKE

Mix dry ingredients together; add butter, water, and applesauce. Beat for 2 minutes at medium speed with mixer. Add eggs; beat for 2 more minutes. Fold in raisins and nuts. Bake in greased 9" × 13" pan for 45 to 50 minutes at 350 degrees. Frost when cool.

ICING

Melt butter in saucepan; add sugar and bring to boil. Add cream. Remove from heat and cool to lukewarm. Add enough confectioners' sugar for good spreading consistency.

CHOCOLATE CHOCOLATE ANGEL FOOD CAKE

Senator Jay Rockefeller, WEST VIRGINIA

12 large egg whites
1 teaspoon cream of tartar
1¼ cups sugar
¼ teaspoon salt
1 teaspoon vanilla extract
¾ cup cake flour (Presto)
¼ cup cocoa powder
¼ cup chocolate syrup

Preheat oven to 325 degrees. Beat egg whites in a large bowl for a few minutes before adding the cream of tartar. Beat until egg whites stand in stiff peaks. Combine the sugar and salt (if using granulated sugar, instead of superfine bar sugar, sift it twice).

Slowly add the sugar to the beaten egg whites and also add the vanilla. Continue beating until peaks are not only stiff but shiny. Sift the flour and the cocoa powder together and fold into the mixture (try to deflate the egg whites as little as possible).

Spoon into an ungreased angel food cake tin. While doing this be sure there are no air bubbles and push the mixture into the sides around the tin. When tin is about ⅓ full, drizzle the chocolate sauce over the surface. Plunge a spoon or spatula into the batter about 3 times for a marbled effect.

Add ⅓ more batter and repeat the previous step, plunging in different areas than last time. Now add the remainder of the batter. Keep in mind that the syrup will settle to the bottom of the tin during baking if you use too much or it is all in one area.

Put tin in the oven on a middle or lower rack (so cake does not brown too quickly) and bake for 50 to 60 minutes. Remove from the oven and turn upside down, using the small feet on the rim of the tin.

(continued)

Place on the counter to cool. It is important to have the cake upside down; otherwise it will be heavy. If your tin does not have feet, use a narrow-neck bottle to fit through the hole of the center of the pan. Let it stay until completely cooled. Run a serrated knife around the inside and outside of the tin to loosen. Also do the same around the bottom of the tin once the cake has been removed from the sides.

Cut slices using a serrated knife in a sawing motion.

Makes 12 to 14 servings.

MELT-IN-YOUR-MOUTH BLUEBERRY CAKE

★

Senator Susan M. Collins, MAINE

   2 eggs, separated
   1 cup sugar
  ½ cup shortening
  ¼ teaspoon salt
   1 teaspoon vanilla
1½ cups flour, sifted
   1 teaspoon baking powder
  ⅓ cup milk
1½ cups fresh Maine blueberries

Beat egg whites until stiff in a small glass bowl. Add about ¼ cup of the sugar to keep them stiff. Cream shortening; add salt and vanilla. Add remaining sugar gradually. Add unbeaten egg yolks and beat until light and creamy. Sift flour with baking powder. Add alternately to creamed mixture with milk. Fold in beaten egg whites. Coat the blueberries with 1 tablespoon of flour and then fold into mixture. Turn into 8" × 8" pan. Bake at 350 until toothpick comes out clean, 45 to 50 minutes for a large pan.

FAVORITE CAKE

★

Representative Henry Waxman, CALIFORNIA

    2   cups apple slices, peeled and diced
½ to 1   cup sugar, depending on tartness of the apples
    ¾   cup safflower oil
    1   egg, beaten
    1   cup flour
    1   teaspoon cinnamon
    ¼   teaspoon salt
    1   teaspoon vanilla
    1   teaspoon baking soda
    ½   cup walnuts, chopped
    1   teaspoon (or to taste) orange rind, grated
    ½   cup currants, plumped in water

Place apples and sugar in a bowl. Let stand 30 minutes or more.
Add and mix oil, egg, flour, cinnamon, salt, vanilla, baking soda, walnuts, grated orange rind, and currants. Blend in apples. Mix well.

Bake in a well-greased 8" pan for about 45 minutes. Cool in pan for 10 minutes.

Serve with whipped cream or ice cream.

KAHLÚA CHOCOLATE FUDGE CAKE

Vice President Joe Biden

PECAN PAN COATING

 1 tablespoon butter
 ¼ cup pecans, finely chopped
 1 teaspoon sugar

CAKE

 ¾ cup unsweetened cocoa
 1 cup boiling water
 ½ cup Kahlúa, divided
 1⅔ cups flour, sifted
 1 teaspoon baking soda
 ½ teaspoon baking powder
 ½ teaspoon salt
 ¾ cup butter
 1½ cups sugar
 3 large eggs, beaten
 3 tablespoons raspberry jam

FROSTING

 6 ounces semisweet chocolate chips
 ½ cup butter
 1 teaspoon instant coffee
 ¼ cup Kahlúa

PECAN PAN COATING

Butter sides of a 9" spring form pan. Spread butter in bottom of pan. Sprinkle with pecans and sugar. Set aside.

(continued)

CAKE

Mix cocoa with boiling water; let cool, then add ¼ cup Kahlúa. Set aside. Mix flour, baking soda, baking powder, and salt together. Set aside. Cream butter and sugar until fluffy. Add beaten eggs. Alternately blend dry ingredients and cocoa mixture into cream mixture. Pour into spring form pan. Bake at 325 degrees for 60 to 70 minutes. Cool in pan for 10 minutes only. Remove sides; let cool.

Pan coating will serve as bottom of cake. Cut cake in half horizontally. Drizzle remaining Kahlúa over each half. Spread raspberry jam over bottom layer. Spread with ¼ cup of Kahlúa frosting. Sandwich cake and frost all over.

FROSTING

Melt semisweet morsels on top of double boiler. Gradually beat in butter and instant coffee granules dissolved in Kahlúa. Beat until smooth.

Makes 12 servings.

Note: Cake should rest overnight.

JILL'S CHOCOLATE CAKE

Vice President Joe Biden

8 ounces (1 package) cream cheese, room temperature
2 pounds powdered sugar
1 teaspoon vanilla
½ cup butter, room temperature
5 squares unsweetened chocolate, melted
½ cup milk, room temperature
2½ cups flour
⅓ cup butter
4 eggs
1½ cups milk
1 teaspoon baking powder
1 teaspoon baking soda
Dash of salt

Mix first 6 ingredients together. Divide this mixture in half. One half will be your icing.

To the other half add the remaining ingredients. Place in 2 round 9" baking pans, greased. Bake at 350 degrees for 30 to 40 minutes. Let cool and ice with other half of first mixture.

This is our family's favorite chocolate cake recipe.

LEMON JELL-O CAKE

Senator Russ Feingold, WISCONSIN

- 1 small package lemon Jell-O
- 1 cup boiling water
- ¾ cup vegetable oil
- 1 package yellow cake mix
- 4 eggs
- 1 cup powdered sugar
- 1 large lemon, juiced

Dissolve package of lemon Jell-O in boiling water. Cool. Add oil to package of cake mix. Beat well.

Add eggs, one at a time. Beat well after each addition.

Add cooled lemon Jell-O. Beat very, very well. Pour into greased 9" × 13" pan. Bake at 350 degrees for 40 minutes.

While cake is still hot, prick all over with a fork. Drizzle powdered sugar mixed with lemon juice over warm cake. Cut into squares to serve.

Makes 24 servings.

This recipe is from my mother, Sylvia Feingold. She has made it for years for many to enjoy.

FRUIT COCKTAIL CAKE

Senator Daniel Inouye, HAWAII

CAKE

- 18½ ounces (1 package) banana cake mix
- 3¾ ounces (1 package) banana instant pudding mix
- 16 ounces (1 can) fruit cocktail, drained with syrup reserved
- 1 cup coconut, shredded
- 4 eggs, room temperature
- ¼ cup vegetable oil
- ½ cup brown sugar, firmly packed
- ½ cup macadamia nuts, chopped

GLAZE AND GARNISH

- ½ cup butter
- ⅓ cup sugar
- ½ cup evaporated milk
- 1 teaspoon vanilla
- 1 cup coconut, shredded, for garnish

CAKE

Mix together cake mix, pudding mix, fruit cocktail syrup, shredded coconut, eggs, and oil. Beat for 2 minutes. Fold in fruit cocktail. Pour into a greased 9" × 13" pan or two 8" × 8" pans. Mix together brown sugar and nuts. Sprinkle over cake batter. Bake in preheated 325 degree oven for 45 minutes. Do not underbake. Cool for 15 minutes.

GLAZE AND GARNISH

Combine butter, sugar, evaporated milk, and vanilla in saucepan. Bring ingredients to a boil. Simmer for 2 minutes. Sprinkle coconut over cake while it is hot. Spoon hot glaze over coconut.

> This is a variation of a recipe from Mrs. Thomas J. McCabe of Honolulu.

CARROT CAKE

★

Senator Carl Levin, MICHIGAN

CAKE

- 1 cup flour
- ¾ cup sugar
- 1 teaspoon baking powder
- ¾ teaspoon baking soda
- ½ teaspoon ground cinnamon
- ½ teaspoon salt
- 2 eggs
- ¾ cup vegetable oil
- 1 cup carrots, grated
- ½ cup crushed pineapple, drained
- ½ cup walnuts, coarsely chopped

FROSTING

- 6 tablespoons butter
- 3 ounces cream cheese
- ½ teaspoon vanilla
- 3 heaping tablespoons confectioners' sugar

CAKE

Put all dry ingredients in a food processor bowl and mix 5 to 10 seconds. Add eggs and oil and mix 30 seconds; mixture will be very thick. Add carrots and pineapple and process thoroughly. Add nuts and process only to distribute.

Bake in greased pan in preheated 350 degree oven about 1 hour.

FROSTING

Process butter, cream cheese, and vanilla for about 20 seconds. Add sugar and continue mixing. When cake is cold, pat frosting all over. This recipe is designed for a food processor; however, it can be adapted to a mixer.

APPLE DAPPLE CAKE

Senator Christopher Bond, MISSOURI

CAKE

3	eggs
1½	cups vegetable oil
2	cups sugar
3	cups flour
1	teaspoon salt
1	teaspoon baking soda
4	cups apples, chopped
1½	cups pecans, chopped
2	teaspoons vanilla

GLAZE

1	cup brown sugar
¼	cup milk
½	cup margarine or butter

No trip to Pike County is complete without a visit to the Stark Apple Orchards in Louisiana. Governor and Mrs. Lloyd Stark were longtime family friends. During the restoration of the Governor's Mansion, Mrs. Stark could not have been more helpful or supportive.

CAKE

Preheat oven to 350 degrees. Mix eggs, oil, and sugar and blend well. Sift flour, salt, and baking soda together and add to egg mixture. Add apples, nuts, and vanilla. Pour batter into greased tube or Bundt pan. Bake for 1 hour, then remove from oven.

GLAZE

In a saucepan, combine brown sugar, milk, and margarine. Simmer 2½ minutes. While cake is still hot, pour glaze over cake in pan. Cool cake completely before removing from pan.

Makes 18 servings.

RHUBARB CAKE

★

Senator Charles Grassley, IOWA

  1   cup sugar
  1   cup sour cream
  1   egg
1½   cups flour
  1   teaspoon baking soda
  ½   teaspoon salt
  3   cups freshly cut rhubarb, chopped
  1   teaspoon vanilla
  1   cup brown sugar
  1   teaspoon cinnamon

Using a mixer, beat together the sugar, sour cream, and egg. Add the flour, baking soda, and salt. Stir in the rhubarb by hand.

Pour into a greased 9" × 13" pan. Top with mixture of vanilla, brown sugar, and cinnamon.

Bake at 375 degrees for 40 to 45 minutes.

Makes 18 servings.

From Esther, who has given my wife many great recipes.

CURRENT RIVER CHOCOLATE SHEET CAKE

Senator Christopher Bond, MISSOURI

CAKE

- 1 cup butter
- ½ cup cocoa
- 1 cup water
- 2 cups sugar
- 2 cups flour, unsifted
- 1 teaspoon baking soda
- 2 eggs, slightly beaten
- ½ cup sour cream
- 2 teaspoons vanilla

CHOCOLATE NUT ICING

- ½ cup butter
- ¼ cup cocoa
- 6 tablespoons evaporated milk
- 16 ounces confectioners' sugar
- 1 cup walnuts, chopped
- 1 teaspoon vanilla

> Always tucked away in a cooler for our float trips on the Current River, this delicious yet easy dessert is the first to disappear at a carry-in supper.

CAKE

Preheat oven to 350 degrees. Thoroughly grease a 15½" × 10½" jelly roll pan. Combine butter, cocoa, and water in a saucepan and bring to a full boil. While still hot, pour mixture over combined sugar, flour, and baking soda. Mix well. Add eggs, sour cream, and vanilla. Mix well. Pour batter into pan and bake 15 minutes. Do not overbake.

CHOCOLATE NUT ICING

Mix butter, cocoa, and milk in a saucepan; heat to boiling point. Add confectioners' sugar, walnuts, and vanilla and mix well. Additional milk may be added to make icing more spreadable. Ice cake immediately after removing from oven.

Makes 20 to 24 servings.

COCOA CAKE

Senator Charles Grassley, IOWA

1½ cups sugar
½ cup shortening
½ teaspoon salt
 2 eggs
¾ cup sour milk or buttermilk
 1 teaspoon baking soda
1½ cups flour
 3 heaping tablespoons cocoa
 1 teaspoon vanilla
½ cup boiling water

Cream the sugar, shortening, and salt. Add eggs and beat.

Mix buttermilk and baking soda and add to creamed mixture, alternately with flour and cocoa. Add vanilla. Finally, add boiling water.

Pour batter into greased 9" × 13" pan. Bake for 35 minutes at 350 degrees.

Makes 24 servings.

This is one of my mother-in-law's favorite standbys. My wife has been making it since she was in high school.

POUND CAKE

Senator Robert Byrd, WEST VIRGINIA

- 2 cups sugar
- 1 cup white vegetable shortening
- 3 cups flour
- ½ teaspoon baking powder
- ½ teaspoon baking soda
- 4 eggs
- 1 teaspoon vanilla or almond extract
- 1 cup buttermilk

Cream sugar and shortening. Sift dry ingredients together and add eggs, flavoring, and half the buttermilk. Beat 2 minutes and add remaining buttermilk. Beat 2 more minutes.

Bake in 2 greased, waxed paper–lined 8" × 3" loaf pans at 325 degrees for 45 to 50 minutes.

Makes 2 loaves.

RAISIN CAKE (DEPRESSION CAKE)

Representative Frank Pallone, NEW JERSEY

2 cups sugar

1 cup butter or margarine

½ teaspoon salt

2 teaspoons cinnamon

1 teaspoon cloves

¼ teaspoon nutmeg

1½ cups raisins

2 cups strong coffee

2 teaspoons baking soda dissolved in ¼ cup hot water

4 cups flour

In a large pot, mix sugar, butter, salt, spices, and raisins. Pour in strong coffee (you may use instant). Bring mixture to a boil.

Continue to boil for 5 minutes. Cool completely and add baking soda and water mixture. Add flour, 1 cup at a time. Mix well.

Pour into a greased 9" × 13" pan and bake at 350 degrees for 45 minutes.

Makes 10 servings.

GOOEY BUTTER COFFEE CAKE

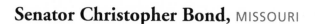

Senator Christopher Bond, MISSOURI

16 ounces (1 box) pound cake mix
 4 eggs
½ cup butter, melted
16 ounces confectioners' sugar, divided
 8 ounces (1 package) cream cheese, softened
1½ teaspoons vanilla

Preheat oven to 350 degrees. Combine cake mix, 2 of the eggs, and butter. Pour into a well-greased 9" × 13" baking pan. Reserve 2 tablespoons of sugar. Combine remaining eggs, sugar, cream cheese, and vanilla. Mix well and spread over batter. Bake for 15 minutes.

Remove from oven; sprinkle reserved sugar on top. Return to oven and continue baking for 25 minutes. Cool on rack or serve warm.

Makes 10 to 12 servings.

SOUR CREAM CHOCOLATE CAKE

Senator John Thune, SOUTH DAKOTA

CAKE

2	cups flour
2	cups sugar
1	cup water
¾	cup sour cream
¼	cup shortening
1¼	teaspoons soda
1	teaspoon salt
½	teaspoon baking powder
2	eggs
1	teaspoon vanilla
4	ounces unsweetened chocolate, melted

FROSTING

½	cup margarine or butter, softened
¼	cup cocoa
¼	cup milk
2 to 3	cups powdered sugar
1½	teaspoons vanilla

CAKE

Grease a 9" × 13" pan. Combine all ingredients and beat on low speed. Beat on high speed for 3 minutes, scraping bowl occasionally. Pour into pan. Bake 40 to 45 minutes. Cool and frost.

FROSTING

Combine margarine, cocoa, and milk and heat till barely boiling. Remove.

Add powered sugar and vanilla.

Mix well. Frost.

Makes 8 servings.

WORLD SERIES BROWNIES

Senator Christopher Bond, MISSOURI

BROWNIES

    2   cups butter

    8   squares unsweetened chocolate

    8   eggs

    4   cups sugar

        Pinch of salt

    1   teaspoon vanilla

    2   cups flour, sifted

    2   cups walnuts, chopped

ICING

    ⅓   cup cocoa

    ⅓   cup butter

    ¼   cup milk

    1   cup confectioner's sugar

    1   teaspoon vanilla

> These brownies got their name because my wife packed a container of them before we boarded a Governor's World Series Whistle-Stop Train for a trip across Missouri on October 21, 1985. A friend from Greene County gets the credit for the brownie recipe.

BROWNIES

Preheat oven to 350 degrees. Melt butter and chocolate over hot water in double boiler and set aside to cool. Beat eggs and add sugar, salt, and vanilla. Add cooled chocolate mixture. Fold in flour and chopped nuts.

    Pour into greased and floured 9" × 13" pan. Bake at 350 degrees for 45 to 60 minutes over pan of hot water.

ICING

Combine all icing ingredients, except vanilla, and boil for 3 minutes. Add vanilla and beat for a few minutes. Pour icing over brownies. Cool and cut into 1½" squares.

    Makes 6 dozen.

SPICY APPLE COOKIES

Senator Charles Grassley, IOWA

½ cup shortening

1½ cups brown sugar

1 egg

2 cups flour

½ teaspoon cinnamon

¼ teaspoon nutmeg

½ teaspoon baking powder

½ teaspoon cloves

½ teaspoon baking soda

¼ cup milk

1 cup apple, grated

1 cup raisins

½ cup walnuts

Cream shortening, sugar, and egg. Sift dry ingredients and add alternately with milk. Add apple, raisins, and nuts. Drop by teaspoon on greased cookie sheet.

Bake at 350 degrees 8–10 minutes.

Ice with your favorite vanilla frosting while hot.

Makes 2 dozen.

KAY'S COOKIES

Representative Kay Granger, TEXAS

2 cups flour
1 teaspoon baking soda
½ teaspoon salt
½ teaspoon baking powder
1¼ cups shortening (butter flavored adds flavor)
¾ cup sugar
¾ cup brown sugar, packed
2 eggs, well beaten
1 teaspoon vanilla
2 cups coconut, shredded
2 cups cornflakes
1 cup pecans, chopped

Sift together flour, baking soda, salt, and baking powder. In a large mixing bowl, cream together the shortening and sugars until light and fluffy. Add eggs and vanilla.

Add sifted ingredients to the creamed mixture.

Mix well for 2 minutes on medium speed. Fold in coconuts, cornflakes, and pecans. Drop by the teaspoonful onto ungreased cookie sheets.

Bake at 350 degrees for 8 minutes or until lightly browned. Cool on baking racks and then transfer to container.

Makes 3 dozen.

Kay's cookies are made from a favorite family recipe. The Grangers and O'Days (Kay's sister Lynn and her family) have been enjoying these cookies for many, many years.

TEXAS SWEETIES

Representative Ron Paul, TEXAS

COOKIES

1	cup butter or margarine, softened
2	cups sugar
3	eggs, beaten
1	tablespoon almond extract
3½	cups flour
1	tablespoon baking powder
½	teaspoon salt

GLAZE

1	cup confectioners' sugar
1½	tablespoons milk
½	teaspoon almond extract

COOKIES

Cream butter and sugar. Add eggs and extract. Mix and add remaining batter ingredients. Form dough into 1½" balls and place on greased cookie sheet.

Bake at 375 degrees for 10 to 12 minutes.

GLAZE

Combine ingredients for glaze. Glaze cookies when they are cool.

Makes 3 dozen.

BISCOCHITOS

Senator Tom Udall, NEW MEXICO

2   cups lard

1   cup sugar

1   teaspoon anise seed

2   egg yolks, beaten

6   cups flour, sifted

3   teaspoons baking powder

1   teaspoon salt

½   cup orange juice

2   teaspoons cinnamon

½   cup sugar

Cream lard and sugar; add anise seed and beaten egg yolks. Sift flour, baking powder, and salt together. Alternately add sifted ingredients and orange juice to first mixture.

Knead well until mixed. Roll out ⅛" thick and cut with your favorite holiday cutter or fancy shapes.

Combine cinnamon and sugar and sprinkle over cookies. Bake in 350 degree oven for 8 to 10 minutes until golden brown.

Makes 4 dozen.

A popular holiday favorite in New Mexico, these tasty treats are splendid.

OATMEAL COOKIES

Vice President Joe Biden

1½ cups all-purpose flour

1 teaspoon baking soda

1 teaspoon cinnamon

½ teaspoon salt

1 cup shortening or butter

1 cup brown sugar, firmly packed

½ cup granulated sugar

2 eggs

1 teaspoon vanilla

3 cups old-fashioned oats

1 cup raisins

1 cup nuts (optional)

Heat oven to 350 degrees. Sift flour, baking soda, cinnamon, and salt together. Beat together the shortenings and sugars until creamy.

Add eggs and vanilla; beat well. Add flour mixture, oats, and raisins and mix well.

Use portion scoop and drop onto ungreased cookie sheet.

Bake 10 to 12 minutes (should be golden brown in color).

Makes 2 dozen.

HUNGARIAN BUTTERHORN COOKIES

Senator Richard J. Durbin, ILLINOIS

COOKIE DOUGH

4	cups general-purpose flour
½	teaspoon salt
1	package yeast
1¼	cups margarine
3	egg yolks, beaten
½	cup sour cream
1	teaspoon vanilla

FILLING

3	egg whites
1	cup powdered sugar
1	cup of nuts, well ground
1	teaspoon vanilla

DOUGH

Sift flour with salt, then add yeast. Cut in margarine; add beaten egg yolks, sour cream, and vanilla. Stir until just blended. Wrap in wax paper and chill while making filling.

FILLING

Beat egg whites until stiff. Gradually fold in sugar, nuts, and vanilla.

Brush pastry board or cloth with powdered sugar. Divide dough into 8 parts. Keep balance of dough refrigerated while working on each part.

Roll out each portion of dough very thin and round. Cut into 8 wedges. Put 1 teaspoon of filling on each wedge and roll up from

(continued)

the broad side. Curl and place on buttered baking sheet, tips down. Bake at 350 degrees for 25 minutes. When cool, roll the horns in, or sprinkle them with, powdered sugar.

Makes 64 cookies.

I first obtained this recipe about 40 years ago when I was a paperboy for the now-defunct *East St. Louis Journal* (the same paper that the late congressman Melvin Price once wrote for as a sports reporter). One Christmas, a customer gave me a box of these cookies, which proved so popular with the entire family that I went back for the recipe. My mother baked them every Christmas.

INDIANA MINT BROWNIES

★

Senator Evan Bayh, INDIANA

BROWNIES

1 cup all-purpose flour

1 cup sugar

16 ounces (1 can) chocolate-flavored syrup

4 eggs

½ cup butter or margarine, softened

MINT CREAM

2 cups powdered sugar, sifted

½ cup butter or margarine, softened

1 tablespoon water

½ teaspoon mint extract

3 drops green food coloring (optional)

CHOCOLATE TOPPING

1 cup semisweet mint-flavored chocolate pieces or
semi-sweet chocolate pieces

6 tablespoons butter or margarine

BROWNIES

In a mixing bowl, beat together the flour, sugar, syrup, eggs, and butter or margarine with an electric mixer on low speed until combined, then for 1 minute on medium speed. Turn mixture into a greased 9" × 13" × 2" baking pan. Bake in a 350 degree oven for 30 to 35 minutes or until top springs back when lightly touched. (Top may still appear wet.) Let cool in pan on wire rack. Meanwhile prepare mint cream and chocolate topping.

(continued)

MINT CREAM

In a small mixing bowl, beat together powdered sugar, butter or margarine, water, mint extract, and green food coloring (optional). Beat until smooth.

CHOCOLATE TOPPING

In a heavy, small saucepan, combine chocolate pieces and butter or margarine. Cook over low heat till chocolate melts. Or, in a small microwave-safe bowl, microwave on 100% power (high) for 1 to 1½ minutes or until chocolate melts, stirring occasionally.

ASSEMBLY

Allow chocolate topping to cool 10 to 15 minutes before spreading on cooled brownies. Spread mint cream over the cooled brownies. Pour slightly cooled chocolate topping over mint layer. Cover and chill for at least 1 hour. Store the brownies in the refrigerator.

Makes about 50 small brownies.

DOUBLE-DIP CHOCOLATE CHIP COOKIES

Senator Christopher Bond, MISSOURI

4   cups semisweet chocolate chips, divided
1   cup brown sugar
1   cup sugar
1   cup margarine
2   eggs
1   teaspoon vanilla
1   teaspoon baking soda
1   teaspoon salt
3   cups flour
1   cup pecans, chopped

Preheat oven to 375 degrees. Reserve 1½ cups of chocolate chips for dipping.

Cream sugars, margarine, eggs, and vanilla until light. Add baking soda, salt, and flour gradually, mixing until smooth. Add remaining chocolate chips and the pecans. Using a measuring teaspoon, drop rounded spoonfuls of dough about 3" apart on a foil-covered baking sheet, flattening each mound slightly with palm of hand. Bake 8 to 10 minutes or until done. Remove from baking sheet; cool on rack.

Melt reserved chocolate chips. Dip half of each cooled cookie in chocolate. Spread chocolate evenly over cookie half. If chocolate is too thick, remove excess with a knife. Place cookies on waxed paper. Cool in a refrigerator until chocolate hardens.

Makes 4 dozen.

Our son, Sam, thinks the extra dip of chocolate makes this a stellar afternoon treat with a cold glass of milk.

SPECIAL K BARS

Senator Byron Dorgan, NORTH DAKOTA

1	cup sugar
1	cup light corn syrup
¾	cup smooth or crunchy peanut butter
5 to 6	cups Special K cereal
6	ounces butterscotch chips
6	ounces chocolate chips

Heat sugar and syrup on stove, stirring until mixture comes to a boil.

Remove from stove and add peanut butter and Special K.

Press mixture in a greased 8" × 8" pan. Melt butterscotch and chocolate chips together. Spread over ingredients in pan. Cut into bars and serve.

Makes 2 dozen.

GERMAN CHOCOLATE
CARAMEL BARS

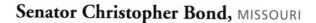

Senator Christopher Bond, MISSOURI

14 ounces caramel

5 ounces evaporated milk, divided

1 package German chocolate cake mix with pudding

½ cup margarine, melted

1 cup pecans, chopped

6 ounces chocolate chips

Preheat oven to 350 degrees. In a saucepan over low heat, melt caramel with ⅓ cup evaporated milk. Combine remaining milk with cake mix, margarine, and pecans. Batter will be stiff.

Press half of cake mixture into a greased 9" × 13" pan and bake for 6 minutes. Sprinkle chocolate chips over crust. Add caramel mixture and spread to edges.

Top with remaining cake mixture. Bake 15 to 20 minutes. Cool on rack, then refrigerate. Cut into bars for serving.

Makes 4 dozen.

Grandmother Ida Doerr Bond is believed to be the source of this family favorite from Perryville.

PINEAPPLE SQUARES

Representative Darrell Issa, CALIFORNIA

FILLING

3	tablespoons cornstarch
½	cup sugar
1	20-ounce can crushed pineapple in syrup
¾	cup water
1	egg yolk, beaten

DOUGH

1	package yeast
1	tablespoon sugar
⅔	cup milk, scalded and cooled to lukewarm
2½	cups flour
1	cup butter
3	egg yolks, beaten

FROSTING

1	cup powdered sugar
4	tablespoons milk
1	cup chopped nuts (optional)

FILLING

Combine cornstarch and sugar. Add crushed pineapple and water and cook on low heat until smooth, thick, and clear, about 5 to 10 minutes. Add 1 beaten egg yolk, mix well, and set aside to cool.

DOUGH

Dissolve yeast and sugar in milk that has been scalded and cooled to lukewarm. Set aside to proof in a warm place. Sift flour and cut in butter, as in making pie crust, until it looks like little peas. Add milk mixture to egg yolks. Combine with flour and butter mixture.

Divide the dough into 2 parts. Roll out to fit a 12" × 14" or 10" × 15" greased jellyroll pan. Place one layer of dough in the jellyroll pan. Spread with pineapple filling and cover with the other half of the dough. Let rise 1 hour. Bake at 350 degrees for 30 minutes until lightly golden brown.

FROSTING

While squares are still warm, frost with 1 cup powdered sugar mixed with 4 tablespoons milk. Sprinkle with chopped nuts while frosting is moist so that they can stick.

Makes 12 to 20 servings.

Note: Pineapple in natural syrup may be used. Increase sugar to ¾ cup for filling.

PIES AND DESSERTS

★ 10

Pies, Mousses,
and Puddings

MICHELLE OBAMA'S APPLE COBBLER

President Barack Obama

FILLING

8	Granny Smith apples, peeled and sliced
	or 1 bag of frozen peeled apples
1½ to 2	cups of brown sugar
1½	teaspoons cinnamon
1	teaspoon ground nutmeg
½	teaspoon salt
¼	cup white flour

CRUST

3	sheets refrigerated pie crust
¾	stick of butter plus ¼ stick melted

FILLING

In a large bowl, mix all ingredients together, cover, and let sit in the refrigerator overnight to let the spices permeate the apples.

ASSEMBLY

Preheat oven to 325 degrees. Butter and flour the bottom of a 9" × 13" baking dish.

Roll out 3 pie crusts as thin as possible. Layer the bottom of the pan with 1½ of the pie crusts and prick a few holes in them.

Pour the apples and the juice that has accumulated into the pie pan. Dot ¾ of a stick of butter around the apples.

Use the final 1½ pie crusts to cover the apple mixture entirely (let the pie crust overlap the pan).

Pinch the edges of the dough around the sides of the pan so the mixture is completely covered. Prick a few holes in the top to let the steam escape.

Brush the top of crust all over with melted butter.

Reduce the oven temperature to 300 degrees. Bake at 300 for up to 3 hours—that's what makes the crust flaky, like Barack likes it. Put the cobbler in the oven and go for a walk, go to the store, or do whatever you have to do around the house. Start looking at the cobbler after 2½ hours so it does not burn.

Not too sweet. Perfect served warm with a scoop of vanilla ice cream. I've been making this cobbler for a long time, so I usually just eyeball how much needs to go in. People might want more or less sugar, but this is how our family and friends like it.

This recipe bakes low and slow, guaranteeing your house will smell wonderful all afternoon.

CRUSTLESS COCONUT PIE

President Barack Obama

¼ cup margarine or butter

1½ cups sugar

3 eggs

1 cup milk

¼ cup self-rising flour
    or ¼ cup flour plus ¼ teaspoon baking powder and
    a pinch of salt

3½ ounces flaked coconut

½ teaspoon nutmeg, freshly grated

1 teaspoon vanilla
    Whipped cream, thin slices of lime or lemon, or
    sprig of mint, for garnish (optional)

Heat oven to 350 degrees.

Cream margarine (or butter) and sugar with mixer, then add eggs one at a time.

Add milk and flour until blended. Stir in coconut, nutmeg, and vanilla.

Pour mixture into a pie pan and bake in preheated oven for 45 minutes, or until golden brown and barely jiggling when moved.

Refrigerate for several hours or overnight. Garnish as desired.

Makes 8 servings.

SOUTH ALABAMA
PEANUT CLUSTERS

★

Senator Jeff Sessions, ALABAMA

2 cups chocolate almond bark
1 cup smooth peanut butter
3 cups miniature marshmallows
3 cups Rice Krispies
2 cups dry-roasted peanuts

Place almond bark in a 3-quart microwavable dish.

Heat on full power for 3 to 5 minutes, or until melted. Stir often. Blend in peanut butter.

Put dry ingredients in a large bowl and pour hot mixture over them.

Blend well. Drop by the teaspoonful onto waxed paper.

Makes a lot!

MOM'S ENGLISH SCONES

Senator James Inhofe, OKLAHOMA

    2   cups flour

    ¼   cup sugar

    ½   teaspoon salt

  2½   teaspoons baking powder

    ½   teaspoon baking soda

    ¼   cup shortening

    ¼   cup currants

    1   cup buttermilk

Sift dry ingredients and cut into shortening. Add currants and buttermilk (dough will be sticky). Knead 1 minute on floured surface and cut into rounds.

Place on ungreased cookie sheet. Bake at 450 degrees for 12 to 15 minutes.

They are delicious while hot topped with whipped butter!

CONGRESSMAN PETER KING'S LEMON SQUARES

Representative Peter King, NEW YORK

1	cup butter
½	cup confectioners' sugar
2	cups flour
4	eggs
1½	cups sugar
4	tablespoons lemon juice
4	tablespoons flour
	Confectioners' sugar

In a 9" × 13" greased baking pan, rub together butter, confectioners' sugar, and flour to make crumbles.

Bake in a 350 degree oven until the edges are golden brown.

Mix remaining ingredients together. Pour mixture over the baked crumbs and return the pan to the 350 degree oven.

Bake for about 10 to 15 minutes, or until the lemon mixture is just about set. (You want the lemon mixture to be a little soft and wiggly.) Cool in the pan.

Sprinkle with confectioners' sugar and cut into squares.

Makes 18 servings.

Enjoy!

JANE SPRATT'S DELUXE PECAN PIE

Representative John Spratt, SOUTH CAROLINA

⅔ cup brown sugar

⅓ cup white corn syrup

2 tablespoons milk

1 heaping tablespoon cornmeal

2 eggs, lightly beaten

   Dash of salt

2 tablespoons butter, melted

1 cup pecan pieces

1 teaspoon vanilla

2 8" pie shells

Preheat oven to 375 degrees.

Mix ingredients in order listed.

Pour into pie shells. Bake for 25 minutes.

Makes 2 pies.

Here's one of my favorites, and a southern favorite as well.

BLITZ KUCHEN

Senator George Voinovich, OHIO

CAKE

3	eggs, separated
2	tablespoons butter
1¼	cups sugar
2	cups flour, sifted
	Dash of salt
2	teaspoons baking powder
¾	cup milk
	Rind and juice of lemon

TOPPING

2	teaspoons cinnamon
½	cup sugar

CAKE

Cream egg yolks, butter, and sugar until light and creamy. Sift and measure flour; add salt and baking powder. Alternately add milk and flour mixture to batter. Beat until smooth. Add rind and juice of lemon.

Beat egg whites until stiff but not dry. Fold in carefully. Pour in a 9" × 13" greased baking pan. Bake 25 to 30 minutes at 350 degrees.

TOPPING

Mix cinnamon and sugar and sprinkle over cake after taking it out of the oven.

Makes 18 servings.

> First made by my wife Jan's mom in 1917!

ZOE'S PECAN PIE

Representative Zoe Lofgren, CALIFORNIA

CRUST

  1 cup flour

     Pinch of salt

     Generous ⅓ cup shortening

  3 tablespoons cold water

FILLING

  3 eggs

  ½ cup sugar

  ⅓ cup dark corn syrup

 1½ teaspoons vanilla

     Pinch of salt

 1¼ cups pecan pieces

CRUST

Mix flour and salt. Mix in shortening until crumbly. Avoid overmixing when adding water. Press into an 8" pie pan.

FILLING

Beat eggs well, then add the rest of the ingredients except for the pecans. Beat mixture well and pour into pie crust.

Add pecans to the mixture in the pan and stir, being careful not to puncture pie crust. Place pie in 350 degree oven and bake for 50 to 60 minutes or until done.

Enjoy!

HUCKLEBERRY PIE

Senator Max Baucus, MONTANA

- ½ cup sugar or honey
- 1 pint fresh huckleberries
- 1 tablespoon flour
- 1 9" pie shell, unbaked
- 2 tablespoons butter

Mix sugar, huckleberries, and flour together. Place in pie shell and dot liberally with butter.

Bake for 30 to 40 minutes at 350 degrees.

The secret of this recipe is the special berries that can come only from the mountainous elevations, chiefly in the West. The taste comes with the eating, but even more so if the person who makes the pie was in on the collection of the berries. They grow with abandon on green wooded slopes just under the tree line and may be accessible only by dirt roads (put there by timber companies of the U.S. Forest Service), preferably on sunny days in late July and early August. The choice spots vary each year, which means that pickers have elaborate games in store either to include or exclude fellow pickers from their favorite slopes. Some people who would entertain a crowd with the results of the day's foray would never dream of revealing the lush and abundant grounds they trod in pursuit of their elusive prize. For these berries—which New Englanders are apt to call blueberries, although the two species do not taste the same to all connoisseurs—are shamelessly shy and do not readily reveal themselves to heavy-footed and acquisitive souls. They require some shade and moisture, and intermittent sun, before they develop their large, smooth, glistening roundness. So splendid and rare a taste they are that black, brown, even grizzly bears also treasure them, and a person may run interference with

(continued)

one or more of these massive creatures when the season is at its height. The higher the elevation, the more likely the bears. So the picker dresses wisely and watches well. He or she may add a tiny bell to the picking can (plastic buckets are best, with large handles) and so warn off the competitors. The bears need to fill up their stomachs in preparation for the long winter's hibernation ahead. The anxious pie lover (or jelly or jam maker, or syrup lover, or any of a number of combinations of these types) only stalks the lonely forests at this peril; but that also gives some added piquancy to the chase. Picking is handwork, unless you fall into the school that appreciates modern marvels and may then choose a carefully crafted wooden box with a clawlike aperture that can swoop through the berry bushes and haphazardly collect bunches that fall back into the receptacle below. But you are apt to collect just as many of the bitter green leaves as well.

Wardrobe is important, too, as is the company one chooses. Always include a foul-weather slicker, in a bright color (those bears again—they are shy, too, and might back off if a yellow or red human being is on the trail), and a rain hat and heavy boots for climbing. Part of the fun is hiking with friends, picnicking in a lovely glen. Part of it is exercise—stopping constantly and talking or singing as you go. The rest of the fun is filling the buckets and then dumping each one into the larger group pot at some central location, then, at the end of the afternoon, carrying home the precious and painfully acquired berries to be divided up among all—and eventually made into pies. Best of all is baking one immediately, for a sort of instant reward, although the berries can be put into tiny plastic bags and stored in the refrigerator, even the freezer. (They can be a very liquid mass after thawing.)

This guarantees that a good pie is a good memory and not just another meal.

LEMONADE PIE

Senator Charles Grassley, IOWA

 6 ounces (1 can) frozen lemonade, thawed
14 ounces (1 can) sweetened condensed milk
 4 ounces Cool Whip
 1 9" graham cracker crust

Mix thawed lemonade and milk. Fold into Cool Whip. Place in graham cracker crust. Chill. If desired, top with cherry or blueberry pie filling.

> Guaranteed to get 'em home for dinner—even a congressman!

SWISH PIE

★

Senator Charles Grassley, IOWA

14 ounces (1 can) sweetened condensed milk
¼ cup lemon juice
½ cup walnuts, chopped
20 ounces (1 can) crushed pineapple, with juice
8 ounces Cool Whip
2 9" graham cracker crusts

Mix milk and lemon juice. Add all other ingredients and place in graham cracker crust. Chill. Garnish with lemon slices or reserved pineapple or nuts.

Makes two pies

This is oh, so good.

CAROL'S BUTTER CRUST

Senator Charles Grassley, IOWA

½ cup butter, melted
1 cup flour
1 tablespoon sugar

Mix ingredients together in pie plate. Press out. Bake until brown, 10 to 12 minutes at 350 degrees.

SAM'S SCRUMPTIOUS PIE

Senator Christopher Bond, MISSOURI

GRAHAM CRACKER CRUST
- 2⅓ cups cinnamon graham cracker crumbs
- ¾ cup butter, melted
- ⅓ cup sugar
- ⅔ cup cocoa, sifted

ICE CREAM FILLING
- 2¾ pints vanilla ice cream
- ½ cup peanut butter
- ½ cup semisweet chocolate chips

CHOCOLATE SAUCE
- 2 ounces unsweetened chocolate
- 3 tablespoons butter
- 1 cup sugar
- 1 rounded tablespoon flour
- 1 cup cold water
- 1 teaspoon vanilla

GRAHAM CRACKER CRUST

Mix together crumbs, butter, sugar, and cocoa until well combined. Press firmly into a 10" pie plate to make solid bottom. Freeze until ready to use.

ICE CREAM FILLING

By hand, combine ice cream with peanut butter and chocolate chips. Spoon into crust. Freeze immediately until solid, about 2 hours or overnight. Top each serving with chocolate sauce.

Note: Do not let ice cream get too soft before mixing with peanut butter.

CHOCOLATE SAUCE

In saucepan, melt chocolate and butter over low heat. Mix sugar and flour; add to chocolate mixture. Add water. Cook over medium heat, stirring constantly until thick. Add vanilla and beat until smooth.

Guaranteed to be a hit with the preschool set and their parents. Combining all Sam's favorite things, this frozen delight is not for weight watchers.

CHIPPED CHOCOLATE PIE

★

Senator Orrin G. Hatch, UTAH

35 large marshmallows

½ cup milk

2 squares bitter or unsweetened chocolate, chipped

½ pint whipping cream, whipped
   or 1 small container Cool Whip

1 10" graham cracker crust
   Chopped nuts, cherries, or chipped sweetened
   chocolate

Melt marshmallows with milk in double boiler or microwave. Cool. Beat well.

Fold in bitter or unsweetened chocolate and whipped whipping cream. Pour into graham cracker crust. Top with chopped nuts, cherries, or chipped chocolate, as desired.

Chill in refrigerator for at least 2 hours.

PUMPKIN TORTE

Senator Charles Grassley, IOWA

CRUST

24	graham crackers, crushed
⅓	cup sugar
½	cup butter

FIRST LAYER

2	eggs, beaten
¾	cup sugar
8	ounces (1 package) cream cheese

SECOND LAYER

2	cups pumpkin
3	egg yolks
½	cup sugar
½	cup milk
½	teaspoon salt
1	tablespoon cinnamon
1	envelope gelatin
¼	cup cold water
3	egg whites
¼	cup sugar

CRUST

Mix crust ingredients and press into 9" × 13" pan.

FIRST LAYER

Mix ingredients and pour over crust. Bake for 20 minutes at 350 degrees. Cool.

(continued)

SECOND LAYER

Cook pumpkin, egg yolks, sugar, milk, salt, and cinnamon until mixture thickens. Remove from heat.

Dissolve gelatin in cold water and add to pumpkin mixture. Cool. Beat egg whites and sugar, then fold into cooled pumpkin mixture. Pour over cooled, baked crust. Refrigerate and serve with whipped cream.

Clipped from a farm magazine, and it's delicious. One of my very favorites.

BAKLAVA

Senator Olympia Snowe, MAINE

PASTRY

1	pound butter
1	pound phyllo dough (strudel leaves)
1½	pounds walnuts, chopped
¾	cup sugar
1	teaspoon cinnamon
	Rind of 1 orange, grated

SYRUP

2	cups water
2	cups sugar
½	cup honey
1	cinnamon stick
3	lemon slices

PASTRY

Melt butter and brush onto a 9" × 13" pan. Place 1 layer of phyllo in pan, allowing ends to extend over pan. Brush with melted butter. Repeat with 4 sheets of phyllo.

Mix nuts, sugar, cinnamon, and orange rind. Sprinkle phyllo heavily with nut mixture. Continue to alternate 1 layer of phyllo, brush with melted butter, then sprinkle heavily with nut mixture until all ingredients are used. Be sure to reserve 4 sheets of phyllo for the top (each to be brushed with butter).

Brush top with remaining butter, trim edges with sharp knife. Cut through top in diagonal lines to form diamond shapes. Bake at 400 degrees for 15 minutes. Lower oven to 300 degrees and continue to bake for 40 minutes. Pastry should be golden brown in color.

(continued)

SYRUP

Cook first 4 ingredients over medium heat on stove until thick. Add lemon slices. Cook 3 minutes. Remove cinnamon and lemon.

While pastry is still hot, cover with prepared syrup and let stand overnight before serving. Baklava should rest for 24 hours before it is removed from the pan. It will keep in the refrigerator for weeks or can be frozen.

Makes 24 pieces of baklava.

A Greek dessert, baklava was introduced to Greece in the sixth century by its Byzantine rulers, Emperor Justinian and Empress Theodora. Baklava is also known as the "sweet of a thousand layers."

LEMON MOUSSE

Senator Christopher Bond, MISSOURI

5   eggs, separated
1   cup sugar, divided
    Juice from 2 large lemons
1   cup heavy cream, whipped
2   teaspoons lemon rind, grated
1   quart berries

In a nonaluminum double boiler, beat egg yolks and ¾ cup of sugar until mixture becomes thick and lemon colored. Add lemon juice.

Cook over simmering water, stirring constantly, until mixture heavily coats the spoon. *Caution:* Do not allow to boil. Remove from heat and cool.

Beat egg whites until stiff and fold into lemon mixture. Fold in whipped cream and lemon rind until mousse is smooth. Chill.

Pour berries into a glass serving bowl and sprinkle with remaining sugar. Just before serving, cover berries with mousse.

Makes 8 servings.

This refreshing and simple-to-prepare mousse is equally appealing when served over fresh blueberries, raspberries, blackberries, or strawberries. Prepare enough for seconds.

CHOCOLATE
MELT-AWAY DESSERT

★

Representative Dan Burton, INDIANA

CRUST

1	cup flour
¼	cup confectioners' sugar
1	stick margarine
½ to ¾	cup pecans or walnuts, chopped

FILLING

2	sticks margarine
2	cups confectioners' sugar
4	squares unsweetened chocolate, melted
1	teaspoon vanilla
4	eggs

TOPPING AND GARNISH

8	ounces nondairy topping
	Chocolate curls (optional)

CRUST

To prepare crust, mix together flour, sugar, and margarine. Press into 9" × 13" pan. Sprinkle with nuts. Bake 15 minutes in preheated 350 degree oven.

FILLING

Beat together all filling ingredients except eggs. Add eggs one at a time; beat 10 minutes. Spread over crust.

TOPPING AND GARNISH

Top with nondairy topping. Chill well. Garnish with chocolate curls, if desired. Cut into squares to serve.

Makes 24 servings.

STRAWBERRY ICE CREAM

Senator Harry Reid, NEVADA

2 pints strawberries
1 cup sugar
1 teaspoon vanilla
1 cup heavy cream
2 cups half-and-half

Puree strawberries in food processor or blender. Add sugar and vanilla.

Add cream and half-and-half.

Freeze mixture in ice cream maker.

Serve.

APPLE PIE

Senator Patty Murray, WASHINGTON

CRUST

3	cups unbleached flour
1	teaspoon dry mustard
¼	cup sugar
½	teaspoon salt
½	cup butter
⅓	cup vegetable shortening
¾	cup sharp cheddar cheese, shredded
½	cup cold water

FILLING

9	tart Washington State apples
¼	cup unsalted butter, melted
1	teaspoon cinnamon
2	tablespoons cornstarch
½	cup sugar
1	teaspoon lemon rind, grated
1	teaspoon vanilla

TOPPING

1	teaspoon sugar
½	teaspoon cinnamon

CRUST

For crust combine flour, mustard, sugar, and salt in a mixing bowl. Blend. Using a blender or your fingertips, cut in butter and shortening until the mixture forms small clumps. Then add cheese until dry mixture has coarse clumps.

Preheat oven to 350 degrees. Sprinkle the water, 2 tablespoons at a time, over the mixture and toss with a fork until the dough forms a ball. Knead once or twice in bowl and divide it into slightly unequal halves. Chill dough.

FILLING

Core, halve, and peel the apples. Cut them into 1" chunks. Combine the apples and melted butter in a large bowl. Add the remaining filling ingredients and toss until apples are evenly coated.

Roll the smaller portion of chilled dough on a floured surface to form a 12" circle. Transfer to a 10" pie plate and press into the bottom and sides of the plate. Trim the dough, leaving a 1" overhang.

Roll the larger portion of dough out to form a slightly larger circle.

Fill the pie plate with the apple mixture, mounding it slightly. Brush the edge of the bottom crust with water. Move top crust over apples, tucking it under the rim. Trim extra dough, leaving a 1" overhang. Seal the edges of the crusts together with a fork and crimp. Trim extra pastry.

TOPPING

Mix the sugar and cinnamon. Prick the top crust in several places with a fork and cut a small vent in the center. Brush the top with water, then sprinkle with cinnamon sugar. Decorate the top with holiday symbols cut from extra dough.

Bake until filling is bubbling and top is golden, about 1 or 1½ hours.

TEXAS PECAN CHOCOLATE CHIP PIE

★

Senator John Cornyn, TEXAS

- 1 cup sugar
- ½ cup flour
- 2 eggs, beaten
- ½ cup butter, melted and cooled
- 1 cup pecans, chopped
- 1 cup chocolate chips
- 1 teaspoon vanilla
- 1 9" pie shell, unbaked

Mix sugar and flour. Stir in eggs, butter, pecans, chocolate chips, and vanilla. Pour mixture into an uncooked pie crust and bake for 1 hour at 325 degrees. Cover the edges of the crust with foil to prevent them from becoming too brown.

Pie is done when a toothpick inserted in the middle comes out clean.

My wife Sandy and I often use this recipe. I hope that you will enjoy it as much as we do.

FLUFFY PEANUT BUTTER PIE

Senator Lamar Alexander, TENNESSEE

⅓ cup butter

1 cup semisweet chocolate chips

2½ cups crispy rice cereal

8 ounces (1 package) cream cheese, softened

14 ounces (1 can) sweetened condensed milk

¾ cup peanut butter

3 tablespoons lemon juice

1 teaspoon vanilla

1 cup heavy whipping cream, whipped

2 teaspoons chocolate syrup

In a heavy saucepan over low heat, melt butter and chocolate chips. Remove from heat. Gently stir in rice cereal until all pieces are completely coated. Press mixture into bottom and sides of a lightly greased 9" pie pan. Let chill for 30 minutes.

In a large bowl, beat cream cheese until fluffy. Beat in condensed milk and peanut butter until smooth. Stir in lemon juice and vanilla, then fold in whipped cream.

Pour mixture into pie crust. Drizzle syrup over top of pie; gently swirl with a spoon. Cover and refrigerate pie for 4 hours or until set. Refrigerate leftovers.

I am a big fan of peanut butter. In fact, when asked about recipes to suggest, my first answer is . . . peanut butter and jelly sandwiches!

CHOCOLATE CHIP CARAMEL BARS

★

Representative Ron Kind, WISCONSIN

18½ ounces (1 package) German chocolate cake mix
¾ cup butter, melted
⅔ cup evaporated milk, divided
1 pound caramel
   or 50 individually wrapped caramels
8 ounces semisweet chocolate chips

Preheat oven to 350 degrees. Lightly grease and flour a 9" × 13" pan. In large mixing bowl, combine cake mix, butter, and ⅓ cup evaporated milk.

Pat half of mixture into prepared pan. Bake about 10 minutes. Cool.

In a double boiler or microwave-safe bowl in microwave, melt caramels with remaining evaporated milk. Spread over cooled layer in pan.

Sprinkle with chocolate chips, then remaining cake mix mixture. Bake 15 minutes until done. Cool.

Makes 24 bars.

CHOCOLATE MOUSSE

Representative Nancy Pelosi, CALIFORNIA

1 pound good-quality dark chocolate, broken into chunks
8 ounces unsalted butter, cubed
8 eggs whites
4 tablespoons sugar
½ cup heavy cream

In a double boiler, melt chocolate slowly; do not boil. Remove from heat and stir in butter until smooth. Set aside and let cool for 15 minutes.

In a separate bowl, beat egg whites and sugar until soft peaks form. Carefully fold egg mixture into chocolate mixture.

In another bowl, beat cream until stiff and then add to mixture.

Chill for at least 2 hours.

Makes 6 servings.

AMBROSIA FRUIT
AND NUT MOLD

★

Senator Benjamin Nelson, NEBRASKA

6   ounces (2 packages) of lime Jell-O gelatin
2½ cups boiling water
1   pint sour cream
1   small jar maraschino cherries, chopped
14 ounces crushed pineapple, undrained
½   cup chopped walnuts

Dissolve gelatin in water. Set aside; when thoroughly cooled, add sour cream and mix well with mixer on slowest speed.

Fold in the rest of the ingredients.

Pour into greased mold and refrigerate for 1 hour.

When ready to serve, place the mold in a pan of warm water briefly to loosen and then turn it into a serving dish.

Makes 10 servings.

DIED-AND-GONE-TO-HEAVEN PEACH PIE

Representative Leonard Broswell, IOWA

¾ cup flour

1 teaspoon baking powder

½ teaspoon salt

1 small package vanilla pudding (not instant)

1 egg

½ cup milk

3½ cups (1 large can) peaches, with juice reserved

8 ounces (1 package) cream cheese

½ cup sugar, plus 1 tablespoon for topping

½ teaspoon cinnamon

Combine flour, baking powder, salt, pudding mix, egg, and milk in a large bowl. Beat for 2 minutes on medium speed. Pour into a 10" greased pie pan.

Place drained peaches on top, then set aside.

Combine cream cheese, ½ cup sugar, and 3 tablespoons peach juice. Beat for 2 minutes until smooth. Spoon on top of the peaches and keep away from the edge—about 1".

Sprinkle 1 tablespoon of sugar and ½ teaspoon of cinnamon on top.

Bake at 350 degrees for 30 to 35 minutes.

CHEESECAKE

★

Representative Jo Ann Emerson, MISSOURI

CRUST

   1½   cups graham cracker crumbs

   ½   cup sugar

   ¼   cup butter, melted

CAKE

   4   well-beaten eggs

   1   cup sugar

   3   large packages Philadelphia cream cheese,
        room temperature

   6   tablespoons milk

TOPPING

   1   pint sour cream

   ¾   cup sugar

   1   teaspoon vanilla

Mix crust ingredients and pat in the bottom of a spring form pan.

Mix cake ingredients until smooth, gradually adding milk. Pour cake mixture into the graham cracker-lined pan. Mix topping ingredients and set aside.

Bake at 300 degrees for 1 hour or until the center is firm. Let cool for 5 minutes. Pour on the topping. Cool for 5 more minutes.

Refrigerate for at least 2 hours before serving.

CHOCOLATE NUT PIE

Senator Mitch McConnell, KENTUCKY

½ cup margarine, melted

1 cup sugar

½ cup flour

2 eggs, slightly beaten

1 teaspoon vanilla

¾ cup nuts (pecans or walnuts), chopped

¾ cup chocolate chips

1 9" pie shell

Mix in order given. Pour into unbaked 9" pie shell. Bake at 350 degrees for 30 minutes or until middle is set.

BAKED APPLES

★

Senator Jay Rockefeller, WEST VIRGINIA

4   Granny Smith apples
2   tablespoons sugar
4   teaspoons margarine or butter
¼   cup raisins
⅓   cup brown sugar, firmly packed
1   tablespoon flour
½   teaspoon cinnamon
1   tablespoon water

Preheat oven to 350 degrees. Take a small, rectangular ovenproof dish and lightly grease the bottom with a little margarine or butter.

Core apples, all the way through, and peel away the skin from around the top of the apple. Slice away a small piece from the bottom of the apple so that it will stand up straight in the dish. Place the apples in the dish.

Mix together the sugar and butter with the raisins and place in the cored-out cavity of each apple.

Place in the oven and bake for approximately 20 minutes. Meanwhile in a small bowl, combine the brown sugar, flour, and cinnamon along with the water.

Spoon over the baking apples and continue to bake for another 10 minutes.

Serve either warm or cool.

Makes 6 servings.

SIXTH DISTRICT APPLE PIE

Representative Howard Coble, NORTH CAROLINA

CRUST

   2   cups flour, sifted
   ½   teaspoon sugar
   ¼   teaspoon salt
   ¾   cup butter or shortening
   5   tablespoons cold water
   1   egg, beaten

FILLING

   1½ pounds cooking apples, peeled and diced
       (yielding 4 to 5 cups)
   6   ounces light brown sugar
   ½   cup raisins
   1   teaspoon cinnamon
   ½   teaspoon nutmeg
   5   tablespoons flour
   ½   teaspoon lemon juice
   ¼   teaspoon vanilla
       Rind of ½ lemon, grated

CRUST

Mix flour, sugar, and salt. Cut in butter with pastry blender. Add cold water gradually and stir just until dough is moistened. Cover and refrigerate 1 to 2 hours.

Place half of dough on floured pastry cloth. Roll to ¼" thickness. Cut 11" diameter circle; place in 9" pie tin. Prick surface lightly and bake 5 minutes in 400 degree oven. Brush with a little beaten egg and bake 1 minute longer.

(continued)

FILLING

Combine the filling ingredients. Place apple mixture in crust. Roll top crust as above and place on top of pie. Trim excess dough and crimp edges to seal. Cut 3 to 4 vents in top of crust, then brush with beaten egg and sprinkle with sugar. Bake 50 minutes to 1 hour at 400 degrees or until golden brown.

CONNECTICUT YANKEE STRAWBERRY RHUBARB PIE

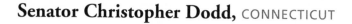

Senator Christopher Dodd, CONNECTICUT

FILLING

1½	cups sugar
¼	cup all-purpose flour
¼	teaspoon salt
¼	teaspoon Connecticut nutmeg, freshly grated
1	cup strawberries, sliced
3	cups rhubarb, cut into ½" pieces
1	tablespoon butter

PASTRY SHELL/PIE CRUST

2	cups all-purpose flour
1	teaspoon salt
⅔	cup butter, plus 2 tablespoons
6 to 7	tablespoons very cold water

FILLING

Mix first four ingredients and set aside. Then combine strawberries and rhubarb with flour mixture. Be certain it mixes well and let stand for about 20 minutes. When ready, pour filling into a 9" pastry shell. Dot with 1 tablespoon of butter. Cover with pie crust and bake at 400 degrees for 40 to 50 minutes.

PASTRY SHELL/PIE CRUST

Combine flour, salt, and butter.

Mix well with a fork. Slowly add 4 tablespoon of water as mixing. Add the rest of the water, if necessary, until the dough is manageable and can be molded into a ball.

(continued)

When this is possible, set aside half the dough for the upper crust or lattice top to the pie.

This should be the last step before baking. With the other half of the dough, roll out a piece large enough to line a 9" pie plate. Prick it with the tines of a fork several times. Bake for 7 to 10 minutes. Fill. Cover. Bake. Let cool.

Serve and enjoy!

MINNESOTA RHUBARB DESSERT

Representative Michelle Bachmann, MINNESOTA

CRUST

    2   cups flour

    1   cup butter

    2   tablespoons granulated sugar

FILLING

    6   cups raw rhubarb cut into ½" pieces.

    6   egg yolks

    ½   teaspoon salt

 1½   cups granulated sugar

    1   cup light cream

    4   tablespoons flour

> Rhubarb is very popular in Minnesota gardens during the summer months. It's a hardy perennial that survives the cold winters well and comes back year after year.

MERINGUE

    6   egg whites

    9   tablespoons sugar

CRUST

Mix ingredients and press in the bottom of a greased 9" × 13" cake pan. Bake for 10 minutes at 350 degrees.

FILLING

Cover crust with cut-up rhubarb pieces. Mix remaining filling ingredients and pour over the rhubarb. Bake 1 hour at 350 degrees.

MERINGUE

Beat egg whites until foamy, then add sugar, 1 tablespoon at a time. Continue beating until stiff and glossy. Add meringue to top of pie. Bake until meringue is light brown, about 10 minutes. Let cool before cutting.

    Makes 12 to 15 servings.

POTPOURRI

★ 11

Snacks and Sauces

RAW CRANBERRY RELISH À LA NORVEGIENNE

★

Representative Tom Petri, WISCONSIN

1 quart (1 pound) raw cranberries, fresh or frozen
1⅔ to 2 cups sugar
Rind of 1 orange, grated

Place washed cranberries in a large bowl with sugar and orange rind. With an electric hand mixer, mix at low speed for 15 minutes.

Let rest 30 minutes then beat again. Continue until the sugar has dissolved completely.

Stir with a wooden spoon for 5 minutes or more and give a vigorous turn for a few minutes whenever you feel like it until the sugar dissolves.

This may take a day or two if you are lazy about the stirring.

Store the relish in a jar (preferably a screw-top jar), and it will keep for weeks.

Makes 1 jar.

This is an old Norwegian recipe. Norwegians use dwarf cranberries, which we call ligonberries. This recipe is an adaptation of the original Norwegian dwarf cranberry recipe.

CRANBERRY-APPLE-PEAR SAUCE

Senator Christopher Bond, MISSOURI

2 pounds fresh cranberries

4 apples, pared, cored, and diced

3 pears, pared, cored, and diced

2 cups golden raisins

2 cups sugar

1 cup fresh orange juice

2½ tablespoons orange rind, grated

2 teaspoons cinnamon

¼ teaspoon nutmeg, freshly grated

½ cup plus 2 tablespoons orange-flavored liqueur

Place all ingredients, except liqueur, in a large saucepan. Bring to a boil, then reduce heat. Simmer uncovered for 45 minutes, stirring frequently until mixture thickens.

Remove from heat. Stir in liqueur; cool. Refrigerate for at least 4 hours. Serve sauce slightly chilled with pork, chicken, or turkey.

Makes 6 cups.

Always included with our Thanksgiving turkey, this festive combination of fruits draws accolades when teamed with a wheel of brie on a holiday buffet table at Christmas.

BAKED FRUIT

★

Representative Steny Hoyer, MARYLAND

    1   jar spiced apples
   20   ounces peaches, sliced
   20   ounces pears, sliced
   20   ounces pineapple chunks
    2   tablespoons flour
   ½   cup brown sugar, packed
   ½   cup butter
    1   cup sherry

Drain fruits, then layer them in an ovenproof casserole dish.

Stir together flour and sugar. Add remaining ingredients and heat until butter melts. Pour mixture over fruit.

Cover and refrigerate overnight. Bake in preheated 350 degree oven for 30 minutes.

Makes 12 servings.

FRENCH MINTS

Senator Orrin G. Hatch, UTAH

4   squares unsweetened chocolate
1   cup butter, softened
2   cups confectioners' sugar
4   eggs
1   teaspoon vanilla
1   teaspoon peppermint extract
    Nuts, for garnish

Melt chocolate in a double boiler over simmering water. Set aside to cool.

Using an electric beater, beat butter, gradually adding sugar (beat about 15 minutes). Add cooled melted chocolate. Beat 5 minutes more.

Beat in eggs, one at a time. Mix in vanilla and peppermint extract.

Sprinkle chopped nuts on the bottom of 24 paper cupcake liners. Fill half full and sprinkle nuts over top. Freeze mints for at least 3 hours.

Makes 4 servings.

Note: For sweeter mints, you can substitute one 6-ounce package of semisweet chocolate chips for the squares of unsweetened chocolate.

MARILYN'S MICROWAVE PEANUT BRITTLE

★———————————————————————————————

Representative Kay Granger, TEXAS

    1   cup sugar
    ½   cup corn syrup
    1   cup raw peanuts
    1   teaspoon vanilla
    1   tablespoon margarine
    1   teaspoon baking soda
        Food coloring (optional)

In a 2-quart measuring container with a handle, stir together sugar, corn syrup, and peanuts (use a wooden spoon, not plastic). Microwave for 4 minutes on high.

Stir again, then microwave for another 4 minutes. Add vanilla and margarine. Stir and microwave for 2 minutes on high. Add baking soda. Stir and pour—fast!! Cool and break into pieces.

My best friend made peanut brittle for us every Christmas. Sometimes her peanut brittle would be delivered in its regular brown-sugar color; other times, it would appear dyed red or green. When Texas Christian University played football in Ft. Worth and she could attend, she'd deliver it in purple. We would eat so much that she finally began delivering one batch for each of my children and one for me. It just wasn't Christmas without Marilyn's peanut brittle.

Marilyn was always trying to simplify her life (and mine!), so she would use no recipe with more than 5 ingredients. When I pointed out that the peanut brittle violated her rule because it had 6 ingredients, she said the baking soda didn't count because there was so little of it. Try to understand that logic!

UNCLE BEN'S SPAGHETTI SAUCE

Senator Benjamin Nelson, NEBRASKA

4	cloves garlic, chopped
3	tablespoons olive oil
1	carrot, chopped
1	stalk celery, chopped
1	onion, chopped
½	green pepper, chopped
	Sausage or meatballs
1½	cups tomato puree
4	ounces tomato paste
¾	cup red wine (not cooking)
10½	ounces beef broth
2	tablespoons lemon rind, chopped
1	teaspoon rosemary
1	teaspoon basil
1	teaspoon oregano

Sauté garlic in olive oil, add carrot, celery, onion, and green pepper until lightly colored. Add meats to brown. Add remaining ingredients.

Simmer all together, covered, for 2 hours.

Makes 6 to 8 servings.

Use this sauce as a delicious accompaniment to your favorite pasta dish.

HONEY MUSTARD DRESSING

★

Senator Michael Enzi, WYOMING

¾ cup olive oil

⅓ cup vinegar apple cider or lemon juice

6 tablespoons honey

1 teaspoon garlic salt

1 teaspoon dry mustard

½ to 1 teaspoon dill weed

Blend all ingredients.

> Goes well with Orange Chicken Salad (see page 23).

MEL'S SATURDAY MORNING APPLE PANCAKES

Senator Mel Martinez, FLORIDA

1   apple, peeled and finely chopped
2   tablespoons butter for sautéing apples
½   teaspoon cinnamon
2   eggs
2   cups buttermilk (or 2 teaspoons lemon juice in milk)
4   tablespoons unsalted butter, melted
½   teaspoon cinnamon
2   cups all-purpose flour
2   tablespoons sugar
2   teaspoons baking powder
1   teaspoon baking soda
    Pinch of salt
½   teaspoon vanilla extract

Sauté the apple in butter, season with cinnamon. Set aside. Preheat a griddle over medium heat.

In a bowl, using an electric mixer, beat the eggs until frothy, 2 to 3 minutes. Turn mixer off and add the buttermilk, melted butter, cinnamon, flour, sugar, baking powder, baking soda, salt, and vanilla extract. Continue to beat just until the mixture is smooth, 2 to 3 minutes more. Stir in the apple mixture.

Lightly grease the griddle with nonstick cooking spray. Make 3" to 4" pancakes. Cook until bubbles form on top and the batter is set, about 2 minutes. Flip the pancakes and cook until golden brown on the other side, about 2 minutes more. Keep warm until all the pancakes are cooked.

Serve with warm maple syrup.

Makes 15 pancakes.

> I have enjoyed making these pancakes on Saturday mornings for my children and grandchildren. I hope you enjoy this recipe as much as my family does.

FAVORITE DISHES OF THE PRESIDENTS

★ 12

Jean-Anthelme Brillat-Savarin, gastronomer said,
"Tell me what you eat, and I will tell you what you are."

MARTHA WASHINGTON'S CANDY

★

George Washington, 1789–1797

1	cup butter
4	cups confectioners' sugar
14	ounces (1 can) sweetened condensed milk
2	cups coconut, shredded
2	cups pecans or other nuts, chopped
2	teaspoons vanilla extract
¼	block paraffin
2	cups semisweet chocolate chips

Line 2 cookie sheets with wax paper. Set aside.

Mix butter, sugar, and sweetened condensed milk in large mixing bowl.

Add coconut, pecans, and vanilla extract; mix well, using a sturdy large spoon. Chill until firm enough to handle. Form into small balls and place on prepared cookie sheets. Chill until very firm.

Melt paraffin in top of double boiler over simmering water. Add chocolate chips and stir until melted. Using a toothpick or candy dipper, dip balls into melted chocolate and place them on waxed paper. Let cool until set.

Store in airtight container.

Makes 8 dozen.

GEORGE WASHINGTON'S EGGNOG

★

George Washington

1 pint brandy
½ pint rye whisky
½ pint Jamaican rum
1 quarter pint sherry
1 dozen eggs
1 tablespoon sugar
1 quart cream
1 quart milk

Mix liquors together first. Separate yolks and whites of eggs. Add sugar to beaten yolks and mix well. Add liquor to beaten yolks, drop by drop first, and slowly beat.

Add cream and milk, slowly beating. Beat whites of eggs until stiff and fold slowly into mixture.

Let set in a cool place for several days; taste frequently.

This recipe was recently found, written in Washington's hand.

MARTHA WASHINGTON'S PIE

George Washington

CAKE

1	cup butter, softened
2	cups white sugar
2	eggs, lightly beaten
1	teaspoon vanilla extract
1	tablespoon unsweetened cocoa powder
2	teaspoons baking powder
1	cup milk
2	cups all-purpose flour
¾	cup golden raisins
1	cup walnuts, chopped
2	9" pie crusts, unbaked

ICING

1 cup confectioners' sugar

½ teaspoon vanilla extract

4 tablespoons milk

CAKE

Preheat oven to 375 degrees.

Mix butter, sugar, eggs, vanilla, cocoa, and baking powder together until smooth; alternately mix in the milk and flour. Stir in raisins and walnuts.

Pour mixture into pastry shells and bake at 375 degrees for 60 to 70 minutes. Do not underbake.

ICING

Combine confectioner's sugar and vanilla. Gradually stir in milk until desired consistency is reached. Spread icing on pie when it is out of the oven and still warm.

Makes two 9" pies.

SHREWSBURY CAKES

George Washington

1	stick butter, softened
½	cup sugar
½	teaspoon vanilla
¼	teaspoon salt
1	egg, beaten
2	tablespoons milk
2½	cups cake flour, sifted
1	cup dried fruit (tart cherries, apricots, or other fruit), chopped

Preheat oven to 350 degrees.

Cream together butter and sugar. Add vanilla, salt, egg, and milk. Mix well. Add flour to butter mixture and mix well. Mix in dried fruit.

Chill dough 1 hour. Place small rounds of dough on a cookie sheet (greased or lined with parchment or nonstick foil). Bake for 12 minutes. Cool.

Makes 3 dozen.

MARTHA WASHINGTON'S COOKIES

★

George Washington

2	egg whites
¼	teaspoon salt
⅔	cup brown sugar, packed
1½	teaspoons vanilla extract
1	cup pecan halves

Preheat oven to 250 degrees.

Beat egg whites and salt until foamy; gradually add brown sugar and vanilla extract.

Continue beating until stiff peaks are formed. Fold in pecan halves.

Drop by teaspoon onto greased cookie sheet. Bake for 1 hour. Makes about 3 dozen.

MARTHA WASHINGTON'S GREAT CAKE

★

George Washington

Take 40 eggs and divide the whites from the yolks and beat the whites to a froth. Then work 4 pounds of butter to a cream and put the whites of eggs to it a spoonful at a time till it is well worked. Then put 4 pounds of sugar finely powdered to it in the same manner; then put in the yolks of eggs and 5 pounds of flour and 5 pounds of fruit. Two hours will bake it. Add to it half an ounce of mace and nutmeg, half a pint of wine, and some fresh brandy.

Modern adaptation of recipe: In making Martha Washington's famed cake, Mount Vernon's curatorial staff followed Mrs. Washington's recipe almost exactly. Where the recipe called for 5 pounds of fruit, without specifying which ones, 2 pounds of raisins, 1 pound of currants, and 2 pounds of apples were used. The wine used was cream sherry. Since no pan large enough was available to hold all the batter, two 14" layers were made and stacked.

Note: The original was one single tall layer.

The layers were baked in a 350 degree oven for 1½ hours. The cake should be iced with a very stiff egg-white based icing, flavored with rosewater or orange-flower water.

NELLY CUSTIS'S RECIPE FOR HOECAKES

★

George Washington

8¾ cups white cornmeal
1¼ teaspoons dry yeast
1 egg
  Warm water
  Shortening or other cooking grease
  Honey and butter

In large container, mix together 4 cups white cornmeal, 1¼ teaspoons dry yeast, and enough warm water to give the mixture the consistency of pancake batter (probably 3 to 4 cups). Cover and set on the stove or counter overnight.

In the morning, gradually add remaining cornmeal, egg, and enough warm water to give the mixture the consistency of pancake batter (3 to 4 cups). Cover and set aside for 15 to 20 minutes.

Add shortening or other cooking grease to a griddle or skillet and heat until water sprinkled onto it will bead up.

Pour batter, by the spoonful, onto the hot griddle.

Note: Since the batter has a tendency to separate, you will need to stir it well before pouring each batch.

When the hoecake is brown on one side, turn it over and brown the other. Serve warm with butter and honey.

General Washington's typical breakfast has been described by members of his immediate family and several guests. His step-granddaughter, Nelly Custis Lewis, who was raised at Mount Vernon, wrote, "He rose before sunrise, always wrote or read until 7 in summer or half past seven in winter. His breakfast was then ready—he ate three small mush cakes (Indian meal) swimming in butter and honey, and drank three cups of tea without cream." She described the recipe in a letter: "The bread business is as follows if you wish to make 2½ quarts of flour up—take at night one quart of flour, five table spoonfuls of yeast & as much lukewarm water as will make it the consistency of pancake batter, mix it in a large stone pot & set it near a warm hearth (or a moderate fire) make it at candlelight & let it remain until the next morning then add the remaining quart & a half by degrees with a spoon when well mixed let it stand 15 or 20 minutes & then bake it—of this dough in the morning, beat up a white & half of the yolk of an egg—add as much lukewarm water as will make it like pancake batter, drop a spoonful at a time on a hoe or griddle (as we say in the south). When done on one side turn the other—the griddle must be rubbed in the first instance with a piece of beef suet or the fat of cold corned beef."

CRANBERRY PUDDING

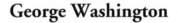

George Washington

PUDDING

2	eggs, beaten
2	tablespoons sugar
	Pinch salt
½	cup molasses
2	teaspoons baking soda
⅓	cup boiling water
1½	cups flour, sifted
1½	cups cranberries, cut in half

SAUCE

2	sticks butter
2	cups sugar
1	cup half-and-half

PUDDING

Combine eggs, sugar, salt, and molasses. In a separate container, put 2 teaspoons of soda in ⅓ cup boiling water. Add to egg mixture. Stir in flour and cranberries. Steam in a buttered rice steamer for 1½ hours. Serve warm with the following sauce.

SAUCE

Melt butter. Add sugar and half-and-half and stir until sugar is dissolved.

Makes 6 to 8 servings.

MARTHA WASHINGTON'S SHERRY CRAB SOUP

George Washington

4 cups warm milk

3 hard-boiled eggs, coarsely chopped

1 tablespoon butter, melted

4 teaspoons all-purpose flour

½ teaspoon salt (more or less to taste)

¼ teaspoon ground pepper (more or less to taste)

1 teaspoon lemon zest, freshly grated

½ pound crab meat, cooked

½ cup heavy whipping cream

½ cup dry sherry

¼ teaspoon Worcestershire sauce

Combine 1 cup of the warm milk with the eggs, butter, and flour in a blender. Puree until the mixture is completely smooth. Add the remaining milk and blend well.

Transfer the pureed mixture to a soup pot and season with salt and pepper. Add the lemon zest and the crab. Heat until the soup is hot but not boiling.

Drizzle the cream into the pot while stirring constantly. Then drizzle the sherry into the soup while stirring constantly. Whisk in the Worcestershire sauce and serve immediately.

8 servings.

In Martha Washington's day, though, crab was extraordinarily plentiful and cream was considered a necessity. Martha Washington's Sherry Crab Soup is one of the few White House recipes that have been consistently made through two centuries of presidencies.

With the help of a blender, you can prepare this soup quickly and easily. It's rich in every way—high in fat, quite expensive, and abundantly flavorful.

MARTHA WASHINGTON'S DEVIL'S FOOD

★

George Washington

4	ounces unsweetened chocolate
1	cup sugar
½	cup buttermilk or sour milk
½	cup cake flour, sifted
1½	teaspoons baking powder
¾	teaspoon baking soda
½	teaspoon salt
½	cup unsalted butter or shortening
¾	cup granulated sugar
3	eggs, well beaten
1	cup buttermilk or sour milk
1	teaspoon vanilla

Melt chocolate in a double boiler. Add 1 cup sugar and ½ cup buttermilk or sour milk and stir until sugar is dissolved. Cool. Sift flour once, measure, add baking powder, baking soda, and salt and sift together three times. Cream butter thoroughly, add ¾ cup sugar gradually, and cream together until light and fluffy. Add eggs and beat well. Add about ¼ of flour mixture, mix thoroughly; add chocolate mixture and blend. Add remaining flour, alternately with buttermilk, a small amount at a time; beat very thoroughly after each addition. Add vanilla. Bake in greased 15" × 9" × 2" pan, in a moderate oven
(350 degrees) 30 minutes, or until cake is done.

When cold, trim edges, cut in half crosswise, and put together as a two-layer cake, matching edges carefully.

George Washington once referred to his home as a "well-resorted tavern" and existing records confirm this description. According to household documents, Mr. and Mrs. Washington dined alone only twice in the last 20 years of their marriage. Friends as well as curious citizens flocked to see the President, and, with customary grace, he welcomed them to his home, not only for meals but to spend the night. One guest described Washington's hospitality as "entertainments . . . conducted with the most regularity and in the genteelest manner." . . .

In 1777, visitor Nicholas Cresswell was equally laudatory: "[George Washington] keeps an excellent table and a stranger, let him be of what Country or nation, he will always meet with a hospitable reception at it."

While the cost of entertaining was considerable, cash was not generally required. George Washington's own farms (covering nearly 8,000 acres) were self-sufficient and could provide most of the produce and meat that was necessary.

Once the dinner bell rang, Washington subscribed to the 5-minute rule: guests must be seated within 5 minutes of the bell. Once everyone was seated, the dishes were placed in the center of the table and in a decorative fashion around the eating area.

And what did guests eat? One visitor from New York recounts the following:

At dinner have wine, porter and/or beer. After it we drank about three glasses. . . . At dinner we had two pint globular decanters on table, after dinner large wine glasses. Port was brought in claret bottles. . . . Menu . . . Leg boiled pork, top; goose, roast beef, round cold boiled beef, mutton chops, hominy, cabbage, potatoes, pickles, fried tripe, onions etc. Table cloth wiped, mince pies, tarts, cheese; cloth of port, Madeira, two kinds nuts, apples, raisins. Three servants.

(continued)

★ ———————————————————————————————————

According to a newly released book entitled George Washington's Mount Vernon (ed. Wendell Garrett), "the Washingtons were among the first colonial Americans to acquire Josiah Wedgwood's fashionable cream-colored 'Queen's Ware' and among the first post-Revolution Americans to purchase porcelains brought back from Canton on the Empress of China, the ship that opened American trade with China."

As cognizant of precedents on the dining table as he was in matters of government, Washington also acquired the nation's first service of French porcelain to grace state dinners, a practice that continued until 1900.

Washington was equally concerned with manners. At age 15, he copied a series of injunctions regarding manners "in company and conversation" which survives to this day. Among those rules are some special admonitions governing behavior at the dining table: "Make no shew of taking great Delight in your Victuals, Feed not with Greediness; cut your Bread with a Knife, lean not on the Table, neither find fault with what you Eat." This superb advice as well as many other helpful tidbits is available in a lovely booklet entitled George Washington's Rules of Civility and Decent Behaviour in Company and Conversation.

When he wasn't entertaining, Mr. Washington generally had breakfast at 7 (7:30 in the winter) and dined on his favorite, hoe cakes—corn cakes topped with butter and honey. He had dinner at 3. Tea was served from 6 to 7 and he retired generally at 9 p.m.

While there is no archival evidence of particular recipes George Washington enjoyed, there are a number of excellent books which highlight colonial favorites or recipes made with ingredients available in colonial times.

Source: A Petri, "George Washington and Food." http:11petri.house .gov/gw003.htm.

GEORGE WASHINGTON'S BEER

George Washington

"Take a large snifter full of bran hops to your taste—boil these 3 hours. Then strain our 30 gall[o]n into a cooler put in 3 gall[o]n molasses while the beer is scalding hot or rather draw the molasses into the cooler. Strain the beer on it while boiling hot, let this stand till it is little more than blood warm. Then put in a quart of yeast if the weather is very cold cover it over with a blanket let it work in the cask—Leave the bung open till it is almost done working— Bottle it that day week it was brewed."

Note: Recipe courtesy Precious Book Department, New York Public Library. Spelling and punctuation have been left in their original form.

Note: Following this recipe exactly will result in a beer with an alcohol content of about 11 percent—making it at least twice as potent as most of today's commercially brewed domestic beers.

ABIGAIL ADAMS'S APPLE PAN DOWDY

John Adams, 1797–1801

PASTRY
- 1½ cups flour
- ½ cup shortening

FILLING
- ½ cup sugar
- ½ teaspoon cinnamon
- ¼ teaspoon salt
- ¼ teaspoon nutmeg
- 10 large apples
- ½ cup molasses
- 3 tablespoons butter, melted
- ¼ cup water

PASTRY

Blend flour and shortening until mealy. Sprinkle a little ice water over dough, enough to hold together. Roll out to ¼" thickness and brush with ¼ cup melted butter. Cut pastry in half. Place halves on top of each other. Roll and cut again. Repeat until you have 16 separate pieces piled up. Then chill for 1 hour. Roll pastry again and cut in half. Line bottom of baking dish with one half. Save other half for the top.

FILLING

Peel and slice the apples. Mix with sugar and spices and put in the pastry lined dish.

Combine molasses with butter and water. Pour over the apples.

Cover with top crust and seal. Bake at 400 degrees for 10 minutes. Then reduce heat to 325 degrees.

"Dowdy" the dish by cutting the crust into the apples with a sharp knife.

Bake 1 hour. Serve hot with ice cream or whipped cream.

ABIGAIL ADAMS'S HOT CRAB SALAD

John Adams

2   tablespoons butter
2   tablespoons flour
1   cup milk
½   pound lump crabmeat, picked over
¼   cup pimentos, rinsed, drained, and diced
½   cup sliced almonds, toasted
4–6 pastry or cream puff shells

Make a cream sauce with butter, flour, and milk.
Remove from the heat and add crab, pimentos, and almonds.,
Serve in prebaked pastry shells or cream puff shells.

This is extremely simple, and although the price of crabmeat makes it an extravagance today, this recipe makes a worthy expenditure.

ABIGAIL ADAMS'S BEGGAR'S PUDDING WITH SACK SAUCE

John Adams

PUDDING

1 egg, beaten
1 cup milk
½ cup brown sugar, packed
1 teaspoon rosewater
½ teaspoon ground nutmeg
⅛ teaspoon salt
¼ teaspoon ground ginger
½ cup dried currants
10 slices stale bread in 1" cubes

SACK SAUCE

¼ cup butter
1 tablespoon brown sugar, packed
½ cup dry sherry
1 tablespoon lemon juice
1 teaspoon lemon peel, grated

PUDDING

In a large bowl combine beaten egg, milk, brown sugar, rosewater, ginger, nutmeg, and salt. Add bread cubes and currants; stir well. Turn into a greased, round 8" baking dish. Bake at 350 degrees for approximately 25 minutes or until a knife inserted in the center of the pudding comes out clean. Serve hot, topped with hot sack sauce.

SACK SAUCE

Melt butter in a small saucepan over a low heat. Stir continuously until butter starts to brown, then remove from heat. Add brown sugar; stir until dissolved. Add dry sherry, lemon juice, and grated lemon peel. Serve immediately.

Makes 6 servings.

THOMAS JEFFERSON'S CHICKEN FRICASSEE

★

Thomas Jefferson, 1801–1809

3 pounds chicken pieces

1 teaspoon salt

½ teaspoon ground nutmeg

½ teaspoon pepper

½ teaspoon paprika

3 tablespoons all-purpose flour

2 cups water

1 cup dry wine

3 tablespoons butter

1 onion, chopped

2 cups fresh small mushrooms

1 tablespoon fresh sage, chopped

1 tablespoon fresh parsley, chopped

1 cup half-and-half

6 cups hot cooked rice

Sprinkle washed and dried chicken pieces with salt, pepper, nutmeg, and paprika.

Brown the chicken in hot oil over high heat in a Dutch oven; remove the chicken when it is well browned. Reduce heat to medium, add flour, and cook the flour until lightly browned, stirring constantly. Whisk in 2 cups of water and 1 cup of wine until smooth.

Return the chicken to the Dutch oven; bring to a boil. Cover and reduce heat to a simmer. Cook 50 minutes. Remove chicken, keeping warm; reserve broth in a large container. Broth may be strained to remove particles.

Melt butter in the Dutch oven; over medium high heat, add onion and cook until lightly browned. Add mushrooms, sage, and parsley. Add broth, half-and-half, and chicken. Cook over medium heat, stirring until thoroughly heated. Serve over rice.

Makes 6 servings.

THOMAS JEFFERSON'S BREAD PUDDING

Thomas Jefferson

1½   pound stale bread, cubed

 4   cups milk, scalded

½   pound butter

½   pint brandy

 8   eggs

 3   cups sugar

¾   tablespoon nutmeg

 2   tablespoons vanilla extract

Preheat oven to 350 degrees. Cut up bread while milk and butter are heating in a pot. Combine liquids, eggs, sugar, and spices.

Add bread last by submerging it using your hands so that it gets thoroughly soaked.

Transfer into a buttered 9" × 13" pan, pouring gently so that bread does not break up too much. Bake until an inserted skewer or knife comes out clean, about 40 minutes.

MONTICELLO MUFFINS

Thomas Jefferson

   4   cups of flour
1½ packets of yeast
1½ cups water
     Cast iron griddle

Mix flour, yeast, and water. Dough will be very sticky. Coat your hands in flour before kneading the dough. While kneading, continue to add small amounts of flour until the stickiness disappears and the dough becomes more solid. You may find you add as much as ½ cup more flour during this process.

Put the dough in a large bowl, cover with a towel, and leave in a warm place overnight. The dough should more than double by morning. The underside of the dough may be a bit sticky; if so, knead it a bit more.

Using your hands, shape the muffins into small golf-ball sized balls. Set the muffins aside, cover with a towel, and let rise for an hour.

Preheat ungreased griddle over medium heat. Add shaped muffins to griddle and cook for about 5 minutes on each side.

The muffins will look like biscuits on the outside and English muffins on the inside.

Serve hot.

THOMAS JEFFERSON'S SWEET CORN PUDDING

★

Thomas Jefferson

16 ounces whole kernel corn, drained
1 tablespoon flour
3 tablespoons sugar
2 eggs
¾ teaspoon salt
¾ cup milk
½ stick butter

Place all ingredients in a blender and mix at high speed for 10 seconds. Pour into a well-greased baking dish and bake for 45 minutes at 375 degrees.

To make enough for company, triple the corn and double everything else and bake it for an hour or more until a knife comes out clean.

Thomas Jefferson was the gourmand—he is even credited with introducing greater American culture to the *île flottante* (which he served at a New Year's fete). Though Thanksgiving was not technically a holiday, he would probably serve something like this sweet corn pudding at his dinner parties during the presidential years.

DOLLY MADISON'S
FAIRY BUTTER

★

James Madison, 1809–1817

2   hard-boiled egg yolks
1   tablespoon orange flower water
1   tablespoon powdered sugar
    Butter, room temperature

Beat and mash the egg yolks until fine grained. Add orange flower water and powdered sugar; beat until you have a fine paste, mixing well.

Combine with equal amounts of butter and force through a fine strainer, with holes, onto a fancy plate.

Dolly brought this to the White House. It was one of those extra touches that she loved!

CREAM JUMBLES

★

James Madison

1 pound butter
2 cups sugar
2 eggs
1 cup cream
4 cups flour
1 teaspoon vanilla (optional)

Cream the butter and sugar together completely. Beat in eggs. Add cream and flour alternately, add vanilla if desired. Chill dough for at least 1 hour. Roll thin; cut into shapes and bake at 350 degrees for 8 to 10 minutes.

Makes about 5 dozen.

MINTED FRUIT CORDIAL

James Madison

2   cups grape juice
2   cups orange juice
12   lemons or limes, or 6 of each
1   cup fresh mint leaves
   Sugar to taste
4   cups cold water

Combine the fruit juices and the mint leaves. Add sugar to taste and chill for 1 hour. Strain out the mint leaves. Pour into a large pitcher or bowl and stir in the water.

Serve with ice and a garnish of mint.

Makes 8 to 9 cups.

THE MONROES' MOCK TURTLE SOUP

James Monroe, 1817–1825

1   pint black beans

4   quarts cold water

½   pound of beef, plus 1 shinbone

½   pound salt pork

2   onions, chopped

2   carrots, grated

1   small red pepper pod

3   hard-cooked eggs, sliced

12   thin slices of lemon

      Salt

      Coarse black pepper

Pick over beans; add water and soak overnight.

Add meat, vegetables, and seasonings; simmer 4 to 5 hours. Remove meat.

When cool, dice the meat and return to the kettle. Puree soup through a colander; reheat.

Serve with a slice of egg and a slice of lemon in each cup or bowl.

Makes 12 servings.

At an 1820 dinner party held in Prince George's County, Maryland, the guests of the Agricultural Society spent the evening singing songs around the punch bowl. President Monroe added to the music by keeping time with his fork.

LOUISA ADAMS'S CHICKEN CROQUETTES

★

John Quincy Adams, 1825–1829

2 to 3	cups cooked chicken, cold
3 to 4	slices ham, cold
2	cups bread crumbs
	Salt and pepper
	Nutmeg, grated
1	teaspoon mustard
1	tablespoon ketchup
⅛	pound butter
1	egg yolk, beaten
	Drippings, for frying
	Parsley sprigs, for garnish
	Radish roses, for garnish

Chop chicken and ham together until very fine. Add half of the bread crumbs, the salt, pepper, grated nutmeg, mustard, ketchup, and butter.

Knead all together well until it resembles sausage meat. Form into cakes. Dip in the beaten egg yolk and coat thickly with remaining bread crumbs.

Fry in drippings until light brown.

Serve hot, garnished with sprigs of parsley and radish roses.

Makes 4 servings.

RACHEL JACKSON'S BURNT CUSTARD

★

Andrew Jackson, 1829–1837

8   heaping tablespoons powdered sugar, divided
6   eggs, separated
2   cups light cream
2   teaspoons almond extract
12   tablespoons coarse granulated sugar

Add 6 heaping tablespoons of the powdered sugar to the egg yolks and beat until very light and creamy. Scald the cream with the almond extract and mix it into the beaten egg yolk mixture. Mix thoroughly. Pour into a round, deep earthenware dish that is large enough so that the cream comes about ½" from the top of the dish. Stand the dish in a shallow pan half-filled with hot water and put to set in a 300 degree oven for 1 hour.

Remove and cool a little.

Now beat the egg whites to soft peaks and slowly add the coarse granulated sugar, beating all the time, and continue to beat until mixture is thick and holds its shape.

Cover the dish with this meringue and pile it up so that it comes up 1½" above the rim of the dish. Put the rest of the meringue into a pastry bag with a small rose tip and decorate the side of the dish only.

Sprinkle the top with what is left of the powdered sugar; put in 325 degree oven for 10 to 15 minutes. Get a skewer red hot and make criss-cross markings on the meringue.

Serve hot.

CHARLOTTE RUSSE

Martin Van Buren, 1837–1841

- 1 cup milk
- 1 envelope unflavored gelatin
- 2 tablespoons cold water
- 4 egg yolks
- ½ cup sugar
- ¼ teaspoon salt
- ¼ cup lemon juice
- 6 ladyfingers, split
- 1 cup heavy cream
  Rind of 1 lemon, grated

Scald milk. Sprinkle gelatin over cold water to soften. Mix together egg yolks, sugar, and salt. Pour hot milk, a little at a time, over the yolk mixture, beating hard all the time.

Cook over a low heat, stirring constantly, until mixture is smooth and slightly thickened. Remove from the heat, add gelatin, and stir until dissolved. Stir in lemon rind and juice, then refrigerate until cold but not set.

Line a 1-quart mold or bowl with ladyfingers, placing some on the bottom and the remainder upright around the sides. Some of the ladyfingers may have to be cut to make them fit. Beat heavy cream until it holds a shape, fold into gelatin mixture gently, and pour into mold. Chill 2 to 3 hours or until firm.

To serve, unmold on a crystal or silver platter or cake stand.

Makes 6 servings.

ROAST WILD DUCK

William Henry Harrison, 1841

- 2½ pounds duck
- ½ lemon
- 1 cup orange juice or orange marmalade
- 1 large orange cut in four with the skin on
- Ground white pepper
- Salt
- 2 garlic cloves
- Lump of butter
- ¼ cup red wine

Remove duck gizzards, livers, hearts, and necks. Scrub fowl thoroughly inside and out, and then rub half a lemon all over inside and out. Dry well on paper towel. Season inside with salt and pepper. Stuff quarters of orange into each duck. Add bruised clove of garlic, and small lump of butter.

Tie up duck carefully and arrange on a rack. Brush with melted butter. Pour a little red wine in the bottom of the roasting pan (save the rest for basting). Roast wild ducks for 25 to 30 minutes in a 450 degree oven; duckling or domestic duck should be roasted in a medium slow oven at 325 degrees for 35 minutes per pound.

Only wild ducks are cooked at a high temperature and served rare.

Baste occasionally with a mixture of orange juice and red wine. Serve carved on a hot platter garnished with oranges and cranberries.

When the ducks are ready dressed, put in them a small onion, pepper, salt, and a spoonful of red wine; if the fire be good, they will roast in 20 minutes; make gravy of the necks and gizzards, a spoonful of red wine, half an anchovy, a blade or two of mace, one onion and a little cayenne pepper, boil it till it is wasted to half a pint, strain it through a hair sieve, and pour it on the ducks—serve them up with onions and sauce in a boat, garnish the dish with raspings of bread.

TYLER PUDDING

★

John Tyler, 1841–1845

¼ cup butter

2½ cups sugar, divided

3 whole eggs

¼ teaspoon salt

½ cup heavy cream

1 teaspoon vanilla

½ of a coconut, freshly grated

2 9" pie shells

Cream butter and half of the sugar well. Beat eggs well and gradually add the remaining sugar, beating constantly. Add salt. Mix in cream well and add vanilla. Stir in coconut and pour into partially baked pie shell.

Baked in low-temperature (300 degree) oven for about 20 minutes, until set.

If you like lightly toasted coconut, reserve some of the coconut from the pie and sprinkle it on the top. If it has not browned sufficiently when the custard is set, run it under the broiler for a few minutes with the oven door open.

TENNESSEE HAM

James Polk, 1845–1849

1 ham
   Cloves
1 cup dark molasses
1½ cups brown sugar
   Cracker crumbs
   Fruit preserves, for garnish

Completely cover the ham in cold water; allow to soak overnight.

Take out and remove any hard surface. Put in suitably sized pot with fresh water, skin-side down; add molasses. Cook slowly (225 degrees), allowing 25 minutes to the pound.

Allow to cool in the liquid.

Pull skin off carefully.

Score ham; stick a clove in each square. Sprinkle with paste made of brown sugar, crumbs, and sufficient liquid to make the paste.

Bake slowly in 320 degree oven for 1 hour.

Decorate the platter with thin ham slices cut from the roast ham, rolled into cornucopias and filled with fruit preserve.

ZACHARY TAYLOR'S DEVILED CRABMEAT ON SHELLS

Zachary Taylor, 1849–1850

> 1   pound crab meat, well picked
> ¼   pound butter, melted
> 12   salted crackers, crushed
> 1   tablespoon mayonnaise, beaten with 1 whole egg
> ¼   teaspoon dry mustard
> 1   teaspoon freshly parsley, minced
> 1   teaspoon Worcestershire sauce
> 3   tablespoons dry sherry
>   Salt and pepper to taste
>   Parsley and lemon wedges, for garnish

Clean and butter 6 to 8 large crab backs or shallow shells or ramekins. Over the cracker crumbs, pour the melted butter, reserving some crumbs for sprinkling over the top of the crabs. Add mayonnaise that has been beaten with 1 whole egg, the seasonings, and the sherry.

Mix in crab meat lightly with fork to prevent breaking the pieces. Fill the shells generously with the mixture but do not pack down.

Sprinkle with the remaining crumbs and bake at 350 degrees for about 30 minutes.

Serve at once with sprigs of parsley and lemon wedges on the side. Makes 16 pies.

Millard Fillmore, 1850–1853

Mr. Fillmore is credited with modernizing the White House. Under his administration, the first iron cookstove was installed. Prior to this time, all cooking was still conducted colonial style, on an open hearth. These modernizations were not immediately embraced by his staff.

We would like to be able to say that Fillmore's single-minded efforts on behalf of the Executive Mansion's new stove were merely indicative of his zest for fine food, his appreciation for gourmet repast, his adventurous eating habits. Alas . . . he had little time for frivolity or luxuries, in dress or food. By the time he was president, his life patterns were established. Plain food, prepared in a simple, farm style, was part of the pattern. . . . Meat, potatoes, and vegetables were the ingredients of life for the Fillmores. . . . Corn Pudding . . . has been a favorite dish of simple eaters such as the Fillmores as well as of White House gourmets. . . . To . . . Millard Fillmore, it was natural that a good hearty soup would often serve as a full meal. . . . Soup to a New York farm family such as Fillmore's was more of a stew of meat, potatoes, and vegetables; when ready to serve, the solids were removed from the soup kettle to a platter. The soup was served, consumed, and then the soup bowls filled with the meat and vegetables from the platter. No sense in wasting time or dishes. . . . [The] Resurrection Pie . . . recipe came originally from the North County of England, home of Fillmore's family. . . . Made by the English settlers in New York State, beef or pork liver and cuts similar to round steak were used.

—Poppy Cannon and Patricia Brooks, *The Presidents' Cookbook* (New York: Funk & Wagnalls, 1968), 202–8.

NEW HAMPSHIRE FRIED PIES

Franklin Pierce, 1853–1857

FILLING

    1 quart dried apples

    1 cup sugar

    1 teaspoon nutmeg

    2 eggs

CRUST

2½ to 3 cups flour

   ½ cup butter

   1 teaspoon salt

   1 teaspoon baking powder

FILLING

Allow 1 quart of dried apples to soak in cold water overnight or for 5 to 6 hours. Drain, put into a saucepan, and cook, with just enough water to keep from burning, into a thick applesauce. Add 1 cup sugar and 1 teaspoon nutmeg. Set aside.

CRUST

Make a pie crust of 2½ to 3 cups flour, ½ cup butter or other shortening, 1 teaspoon salt, and 1 teaspoon baking powder. Dough should be firm and have body. Roll it out and cut it into pieces each as wide as a butter plate.

ASSEMBLY

Beat 2 eggs into the applesauce and place 4 tablespoons applesauce in the center of each crust portion. Fold the dough over (like a turnover)

(*continued*)

and press the edges firmly. Bring deep fat to heat in a deep kettle. Drop the pies into the boiling fat (360 degrees) and cook 4 to 5 minutes, turning so the whole pie is well browned. Best served hot, but may be reheated.

Note: Boiling fat is very dangerous. Adult supervision is strongly recommended.

> This regional specialty was as much a favorite with the Pierce family as the state's ubiquitous maple syrup.
>
> Franklin Pierce was not noted for his fondness of food. Family entertaining was nonexistent. State dinners were not considered "up to par" by Washington's high society.
>
> Pierce . . . was said to be "quiet in his tastes." Preferences for the solid, traditional fare of his native New Hampshire were strong in him. The good, hearty, often quite inventive dishes of midcentury New Hampshire found favor with this native son.
>
> —Poppy Cannon and Patricia Brooks, *The Presidents' Cookbook* (New York: Funk & Wagnalls, 1968), 212.

MASHED POTATOES

James Buchanan, 1857–1861

- 3 large Idaho potatoes
- 1 tablespoon salt, plus extra for seasoning
- ¼ teaspoon pepper
- 2 ounces butter
- 2 eggs
- Pastry bag with rose tube

Peel the potatoes and cut in half. Place in a pan and cover with cold water. Add 1 tablespoon salt. Bring to a boil.

Let the potatoes simmer until they are soft, then drain. Return them to the pan to dry a little. Beat until smooth, adding butter and 1 egg. Season to taste with salt and pepper.

Fill a pastry bag with the potato mixture.

Use a rose tube. Pipe large rosettes on a buttered baking dish; sprinkle with beaten egg.

Brown under the broiler, watching carefully so that they do not get too brown.

MARY TODD LINCOLN'S VANILLA-ALMOND CAKE

Abraham Lincoln, 1861–1865

CAKE

1½	cups granulated sugar
1	cup butter
1	teaspoon vanilla extract
2¾	cups cake flour, sifted
1	teaspoon baking powder
1⅓	cups milk
1	cup almonds, finely chopped
6	egg whites, stiffly beaten

WHITE FROSTING

1	cup sugar
⅓	cup water
¼	teaspoon cream of tartar
2	egg whites
1	teaspoon vanilla extract
	Dash of salt

CAKE

Cream together sugar, butter, and vanilla extract.

Stir together the cake flour and baking powder; add to creamed mixture alternately with milk. Stir in almonds.

Gently fold in the egg whites.

Pour into 2 greased and lightly floured 9" × 1½" round baking pans.

Bake at 375 degrees for 28 to 30 minutes. Cool 10 minutes; remove from pans. Fill and frost with White Frosting.

WHITE FROSTING

In a saucepan, combine 1 cup sugar, ⅓ cup water, ¼ teaspoon cream of tartar, and a dash of salt. Bring the mixture to boiling, stirring until the sugar dissolves.

In a mixing bowl place 2 egg whites; very slowly pour the hot sugar syrup over them, beating constantly with an electric mixer until stiff peaks form, about 7 minutes. Beat in 1 teaspoon vanilla extract.

Serves 12.

"Best I ever ate," is what Abraham Lincoln had to say about this velvet crumbed white cake made with finely grated blanched almonds. No small praise, considering Lincoln's unconcern for food. It is a recipe Mary Todd's family obtained from a Lexington, Kentucky, caterer named Giron, who had created the recipe in 1825 on the occasion of Lafayette's visit to Lexington. Mary served the cake often during the Lincoln's Illinois days and later at the White House.

In those days, the almonds would have been painstakingly grated by hand, one at a time. They can be done in a trice today in an electric blender or, better still, with one of the small rotary hand graters, which give the grated nuts a fluffiness akin to that of flour. One can only wonder what Mary Todd Lincoln's reaction to such modern gadgets would be.

ABRAHAM LINCOLN'S SCALLOPED OYSTERS

★

Abraham Lincoln

¼ cup butter, melted

2 cups coarse cracker crumbs

2 dozen oysters, scrubbed, shucked, and drained, with liquid reserved

¼ teaspoon pepper

⅓ cup cream

2 tablespoons sherry

1 teaspoon Worcestershire sauce

Mix melted butter and cracker crumbs together; sprinkle a third of the mixture evenly on the bottom of a greased shallow baking dish. Add a layer of half of the oysters.

Stir together the pepper, cream, reserved oyster liquid, sherry, and Worcestershire sauce; pour half of the sauce mixture over the oysters.

Add another third of the butter and crumb mixture to the baking dish and top with the remaining oysters. Spoon or pour on the remaining sauce. Sprinkle the remaining crumb mixture over the top and bake at 425 degrees for 10 to 15 minutes, or until crumbs are lightly browned.

Makes 6 servings.

STUFFED EGGPLANT, SPANISH STYLE

Andrew Johnson, 1865–1869

4   small, firm eggplants, well washed
1   cup celery heart, including tops, chopped
1   large can solid-pack tomatoes
    or 2½ cups peeled fresh tomatoes, chopped
1   teaspoon basil
½   teaspoon sugar
1   onion, finely chopped
    Butter
    Herb-seasoned bread crumbs
    or prepared dressing mix
    Salt and pepper to taste
    Tomatoes and broiled back to garnishs

Cut eggplants in half lengthwise, leaving the stem, if any. Using a curved grapefruit knife, cut out the center, leaving about ½" in the shell. Butter the shells well and place them in shallow baking dish or casserole containing about ½" water. Cut the center of eggplant that you have removed into small pieces in a saucepan, discarding any coarse, seedy portions. Add celery, tomatoes, basil, and sugar; simmer over low heat. Sauté onion in butter; add to the mixture. Stir constantly until tender and until mixture is thick.

Place the mixture in the eggplant shells, sprinkle with crumbs, and dot generously with butter. Bake at 325 degrees for about 15 minutes. Drain water, if any, from the bottom of the casserole and serve from it.

Garnish with thin slices of fresh tomatoes and a strip of broiled bacon on top of each serving.

Makes 8 servings.

Note: Large eggplants may be used if small ones are not available. Cut each in half and serve to make 8 portions.

RICE PUDDING WITH LEMON SAUCE

Ulysses S. Grant, 1869–1877

RICE PUDDING

3	cups hot cooked rice
1	tablespoon butter or margarine
4	eggs, separated
2	cups half-and-half
2	cups milk
½	cup sugar
1	tablespoon lemon peel, grated
1	teaspoon pure vanilla extract
⅛	teaspoon salt

LEMON SAUCE

½	cup sugar
1	tablespoon cornstarch
⅛	teaspoon salt
1	cup boiling water
1	tablespoon butter or margarine
1	tablespoon lemon peel, grated
3	tablespoons fresh lemon juice

RICE PUDDING

Preheat oven to 350 degrees. Stir butter into rice.

Beat egg yolks; add half-and-half, milk, sugar, lemon peel, vanilla, and salt.

Add yolk mixture to rice; fold in egg whites that have been beaten until stiff but not dry.

Turn into a buttered, shallow 2-quart baking dish; set in a pan of hot water. Bake 1 hour, or until knife inserted near center comes out clean. Serve warm with lemon sauce.

LEMON SAUCE

Combine sugar, cornstarch, and salt; stir in water gradually.

Cook, stirring constantly, about 5 minutes. Blend in remaining ingredients.

ULYSSES GRANT'S LEMON PIE

Ulysses S. Grant

2	eggs
½	cup lemon juice
2	teaspoons lemon zest, grated
1¼	cups sugar
¼	teaspoon salt
1	cup raisins
¼	cup water
⅓	cup coconut, shredded
2	9" pie crusts

Preheat oven to 450 degrees.

Beat eggs lightly. Add all remaining ingredients, except the pie crust. Mix well. Line the bottom of a pie pan with half of the pastry dough. Pour filling into the pan. Put the top crust on the pie and crimp the edges together. Prick the top crust in a decorative pattern. Bake 15 minutes at 450 degrees; then reduce the heat to 300 degrees and bake for an additional 20 to 25 minutes.

Mrs. Grant admitted that she could not cook, so there is some question as to whether this is her recipe. In her memoirs she confesses,

> Just before the Centennial Exposition, some ladies wanted to get up a cookbook and wrote to me for an original recipe. I did not know what to do. The cake I had obtained from a cookbook and the jelly I had considerable help with, and I was forced to ask the advice of a friend, who advised me to tell these ladies that I did not have an original recipe, did not know much about these matters and had always depended on my cook.

She may have not been able to cook, but Mrs. Grant had a flair for entertaining. Elegant dinners were prepared with the help of the White House chef. The day of Grant's second inauguration was one of the coldest in inaugural history. The parade band had to stop playing because the condensation from their breath caused the instrument valves to freeze. At the ball that night, 6,000 guests were expected but only 3,000 attended. The building was so cold that guests wore their coats while dancing. Canaries had been brought in to add their voices to the dance music, but most of them froze in their cages.
A lavish feast had been laid out—roasted turkey, chicken, beef, ham, mutton, quail, partridges, lobster, salmon, scallops, oysters, and stuffed boars' heads—but unfortunately, most of the food froze before it could be eaten. The guests drank hot cocoa and coffee instead of champagne, and many left early.

Source: Bostwick, Lucy. 1887. *Margery Daw in the Kitchen and What She Learned There.* Auburn, NY.

BOSTON CREAM PIE FROM THE OMNI PARKER HOUSE

Rutherford B. Hayes, 1877–1881

SPONGE CAKE (FOR 10" PAN)

- 7 eggs, separated
- 1 cup sugar
- 1 cup flour
- 1 ounce butter, melted

In two bowls, separate egg yolks and whites. Add half of the sugar to each bowl. Beat both until both form peaks. When stiff, fold the whites into the yolk mixture.

Gradually add flour, mixing with a wooden spatula. Mix in the butter. Pour this mixture into a 10" greased cake pan. Bake at 350 degrees for about 20 minutes or until sponge is golden. Remove from oven and allow to cool fully.

PASTRY CREAM

- 1 tablespoon butter
- 2 cups milk
- 2 cups light cream
- ½ cup sugar
- 3½ tablespoons cornstarch
- 6 eggs
- 1 teaspoon dark rum

Bring butter, milk, and light cream to a boil in a saucepan. While this mixture is cooking, combine the sugar, cornstarch, and eggs in a bowl and whip until ribbons form. When the cream, milk, butter mixture reach the boiling point, whisk in the egg mixture and cook to boiling. Boil for one minute. Pour into a bowl and cover the surface with plastic wrap. Chill overnight if possible. Once chilled, whisk to smooth out and flavor with dark rum.

CHOCOLATE ICING

- 6 ounces fondant
- 3 ounces semisweet chocolate, melted

Warm six ounces of white fondant over boiling water to approximately 105 degrees. Add melted chocolate.

WHITE FONDANT

5 ounces fondant

Warm 5 ounces of white fondant over boiling water to approximately 105 degrees. Thin with water if necessary. Place in a piping bag with a ⅛" tip.

Spread thin layer of chocolate fondant icing on the top of the cake. Follow immediately with spiral lines starting from the center of the cake, using the white fondant in the pastry bag. Start the white lines with the point of a paring knife, starting at the center and pulling outward to the edge. Press on toasted almonds.

SUBSTITUTION FOR FONDANT ICING
CHOCOLATE ICING

- 6 ounces semisweet chocolate, melted
- 2 ounces warm water

Melt the chocolate. Combine with warm water.

WHITE ICING

- 1 cup confectioner's sugar
- 1 teaspoon sugar corn syrup
- 1 teaspoon water

(*continued*)

Combine ingredients and water to approximately 105 degrees. Adjust the consistency with water. It should flow freely from the pastry bag.

ASSEMBLY PROCEDURES

Level the sponge cake off at the top using a slicing knife. Cut the cake into two layers. Spread the flavored pastry cream over one layer. Top with the second cake layer. Reserve a small amount of the pastry cream to spread on sides to adhere to almonds. Top the cake with chocolate icing as described. Spread sides of cake with a thin coating of the reserved pastry cream. Press on toasted almonds.

CORN SOUP

Rutherford B. Hayes

4 to 6	ears of corn (to make 2 cups of corn and corn milk)
4	tablespoons butter, divided
1	jalapeno pepper, finely chopped
2	tablespoons flour
3½	cups milk
1	small onion, stuck with 3 whole cloves
½	cup heavy cream
	Chicken stock concentrate for 2 cups (either soup base or bouillon cube)
	Pinch of sugar
	Salt and pepper

Shuck and desilk the corn. Cut the kernels of each thinly with a sharp knife into a bowl, then, with the flat of the blade, press out all the remaining milk of the cob into the same bowl. Set aside.

Melt 2 tablespoons of the butter in a saucepan, scrape in the jalapeno pepper, and sauté over medium high heat until the pepper is soft. Add the flour and cook, stirring, for several minutes. Gradually stir in the milk/stock combination and bring to a boil. Pop in the clove-studded onion. Reduce the heat and simmer for 5 minutes.

Add the corn mixture; stir in the cream and sugar; season to taste. Return to a boil, then reduce the heat and simmer gently for about 30 minutes.

When ready to serve, remove the cloved onion, stir in the remaining 2 tablespoons of butter, ladle into bowls, and serve immediately.

LUCY HAYES'S MASHED POTATO PUFFS

★

Rutherford B. Hayes

2 cups cold mashed potatoes
2 tablespoons butter, melted
¼ teaspoon salt
¼ teaspoon pepper
2 eggs, well beaten
6 tablespoons cream
Bread crumbs
Butter

Mix the cold mashed potatoes, melted butter, salt, and pepper to a fine, light and creamy condition; then add the eggs (well beaten separately) and cream. Beat it all well and lightly together.

Shape the mixture into suitably sized portions and roll in bread crumbs. Place in a greased pan with butter over each puff, and brown at 400 to 450 degrees, turning once. Serve hot. Goes well with roast.

Makes 6 servings.

WHITE LOAF BREAD

James Garfield, 1881

  1   packet yeast, crumbled over 1 tablespoon sugar
1½ tablespoons lard or unsalted butter
  1   cup hot water
  1   tablespoon sugar
2½ teaspoons salt
  1   cup milk, scalded
6½ cups bread flour

Crumble yeast cake over sugar and let it stand to liquefy. Put lard or butter in a large mixing bowl; add hot water, 1 tablespoon sugar, salt, and scalded milk. Cool to lukewarm (85 degrees). Add the yeast mixture and mix well. Sift in half of the flour, beating well.

Now add the remainder of the flour, mixing by hand. When the dough begins to leave the sides of bowl, turn it out on a lightly floured pastry cloth or board. Cover with a cloth and let stand for 10 to 15 minutes.

Knead by folding the dough toward you and pressing with the heel of the hand, giving a slight turn. Repeat until the dough becomes smooth, elastic, and satiny. Air blisters will appear, and the dough will no longer stick to the board. Knead lightly for about 10 minutes, then shape into a large ball.

Grease the large bowl well with lard and turn the ball of dough over in it to cover the surface with grease. Cover with a damp cloth and set to rise in an area free from draft. At a temperature of 75 to 80 degrees, it should rise.

If the room should be cold, place the dough on a rack above warm water. Allow it to double in bulk, but do not let it overrise or you will have sour, coarse bread. The rising takes about 2 hours.

(continued)

Now punch the dough down with a floured fist. Work the edges to the center, and turn the bottom to the top. Turn it out on board and divide into 4 equal portions. Shape by turning the edges under and leave on the board covered with a cloth for another 10 minutes.

Take 2 heavy loaf pans (5" × 9"); shape the twin loaves by folding the edges under and molding into rectangles. Place dough in pans.

Preheat the oven to 450 degrees. Again cover the loaves with a damp cloth and let the dough rise in a warm place until it is not quite double in bulk. Bake for 10 minutes; then reduce the heat to 350 degrees and bake for 30 minutes longer. When done, the bread should shrink from the sides of the pan. Before removing it from the oven, brush the crust lightly with melted butter. Close the oven door and in a few minutes remove the bread from the oven. Let it stand for a few minutes and turn out on a rack in a warm place away from drafts.

Makes 2 double loaves.

CHESTER ARTHUR'S ROCKS

Chester A. Arthur, 1881–1885

⅔ cup butter
1 cup light brown sugar, packed
2 eggs
2 cups flour
½ teaspoon ground cloves
1½ teaspoon cinnamon
1 teaspoon baking powder
1¼ tablespoon hot water
1 cup dates, finely chopped
1 cup nuts of choice, chopped
1 cup raisins

Preheat oven to 375 degrees. In a large bowl, cream the butter with the sugar and add eggs one at a time. Beat until light and fluffy.

In a separate bowl, stir in flour, cloves, and cinnamon. Add flour to butter and egg mixture, beating lightly.

Dissolve baking powder in hot water, add to dough, and mix well. Add in dates, nuts, and raisins, mixing well. Drop onto greased baking sheet by teaspoonfuls. Cool.

Bake 10 to 12 minutes.

Makes several dozen.

(continued)

If gourmetship were the chief ingredient in presidential greatness, our twenty-first president would score near the top. Few presidents have ever equaled Chester Alan Arthur in social and culinary style. Only one, the master of all—Thomas Jefferson—surpassed him. . . . On December 7, 1881, Arthur took up residence in the White House and celebrated his arrival with a cozy, intimate dinner in . . . [the private dining room]. . . . We have no record of that first small dinner . . . other than the knowledge it was prepared by the French chef Arthur brought with him to Washington. The chef had worked for New York gourmets and was well acquainted with the elaborate dinners of the haute monde of the day. . . . The president's daily schedule stressed moderation. He usually arose about nine-thirty, had a light Continental breakfast of coffee and a roll as he dressed, and then went to his office. . . . Lunch consisted of oatmeal, fish, and fruit—no meat or heavy side dishes. . . . Dinner was at six. He dined lightly, but with style. His favorite meal was a mutton chop with a glass of ale, or a slice of rare roast beef with hot baked potatoes and fruits. Accompanying this was a glass of claret. . . . President Arthur was fond of seafood of all kinds. . . . He was particularly keen on [Rhode Island eels]. . . . He went to the Thousand Islands and particularly enjoyed salmon fishing—and salmon eating. . . . Arthur favored [macaroni pie with oysters]. . . . At Chester Arthur's sumptuous dinners [turtle steak] . . . was just one of the many specialties of his chef.

—Poppy Cannon and Patricia Brooks, *The Presidents' Cookbook* (New York: Funk & Wagnalls, 1968), 302–19.

WHITE CAKE AND FROSTING

Grover Cleveland, 1885–1889 and 1893–1897

CAKE

1	cup butter
3	cups sugar
1	cup milk
12	egg whites, beaten
3	tablespoons baking powder
1	cup cornstarch
3	cups flour
3	teaspoons vanilla extract

WHITE FROSTING

2	egg whites
1	cup confectioners' sugar
½	teaspoon vanilla or almond extract
	Crystallized violets, roses, and leaves, for decoration

CAKE

Cream butter with sugar. To this add milk, then the beaten egg whites. Put baking powder into cornstarch and add flour.

Now gradually beat in flour mixture and flavor with vanilla. Beat all together thoroughly.

Put the mixture into three round 9" cake pans that have been buttered after being lined with parchment paper, also well buttered.

Preheat oven to 350 degrees and bake in this moderate oven for 25 to 30 minutes. Take out of oven; allow cooling in pans.

WHITE FROSTING

Beat the egg whites until stiff, then add the sugar gradually. Continue beating until the mixture is smooth and light. Add flavoring and mix well. Use varicolored crystallized fruits flowers and leaves for decoration.

If desired, this cake can be covered with whipped cream.

CAROLINE HARRISON'S
SAUSAGE ROLLS

Benjamin Harrison, 1889–1893

 2 cups flour, sifted
2½ teaspoons baking powder
 1 teaspoon salt
¼ cup shortening
¾ cup milk
    Sausage, cut into pieces

Make a biscuit dough by combining all the ingredients, except the sausage.

Roll the dough out thin; cut into shapes with a biscuit cutter.

In the center of each dough shape, place a piece of sausage the size of a good-sized hickory nut; roll it up in the dough.

Preheat the oven to 450 degrees and bake sausage rolls for 10 to 15 minutes.

THE MCKINLEYS' BREAKFAST

William McKinley, 1897–1901

Bacon

FRIED EGGS

Butter or bacon fat

Eggs

Salt and pepper

JOHNNY CAKES

⅓ cup sugar

1 egg, whole

⅛ pound butter, melted

1 cup sour milk

1 teaspoon soda

¾ cup corn meal

1 teaspoon salt

1 cup flour

FRIED POTATOES

3 medium-sized potatoes

3 ounces salted butter, divided

¼ teaspoon salt

⅛ teaspoon freshly ground white pepper

1 tablespoon rosemary or thyme, crushed

BACON

One way to prepare bacon is to lay the strips in a cold frying pan and cook over a moderate flame until the bacon is the desired light golden color. Turn the strips frequently and pour off the excess melted bacon fat. Save the fat for drippings. Drain the golden brown bacon strips on paper towels. Serve hot.

(continued)

Another good way to prepare bacon is by oven broiling. Lay bacon slices on a cold broiler rack, 5" to 6" below the heat. Broil until the bacon is the desired light golden color. Turn and broil on the other side. Drain the gold brown bacon strips on paper towels. Serve hot.

FRIED EGGS

Heat the butter or bacon fat in a frying pan. Slip in the eggs whole. Cook as many eggs at one time as will fill the pan without touching one another. Cook slowly. Cover the pan as soon as the eggs have been added, and turn heat very low. Salt and pepper to taste.

JOHNNY CAKES

Mix thoroughly the sugar, egg, and about a third of the melted butter. Use the rest of the butter to grease the griddle. Add sour milk and soda, then corn meal, salt, and flour. Allow to stand in a cool place for ½ hour.

Heat the griddle and test it to see if the butter spits. Rub the griddle with a little melted butter. Spoon out the mixture onto the hot griddle in tablespoonfuls. Brown on one side; turn over and brown on the other. Serve at once, hot, with maple syrup, honey, or jam.

FRIED POTATOES

Peel the potatoes and put them into a pan so that they are just covered with cold water. Bring them slowly to a boil. Drain; chill; cut in half lengthwise, then cut into slices.

Heat 2½ ounces of the salted butter in a heavy skillet, holding out the rest for later. When the butter is foaming, put in the sliced potatoes. Shake over medium heat until the potatoes are golden brown all over. Now add another small lump of butter, salt, freshly ground white pepper, and a tablespoon of crushed rosemary or thyme.

Serve hot.

CLOVE CAKE

★

Theodore Roosevelt, 1901–1909

½ cup of butter

2 eggs, whole

½ cup of molasses, mixed with 1 teaspoon soda

2 cups flour

½ teaspoon each cloves, cinnamon, and allspice

1½ teaspoons nutmeg

3 cups seedless raisins

½ pound crystallized ginger and butter, for garnish

Mix butter and milk; add eggs, beating well. Add molasses and soda, and flour that has been sifted together with the spices. Beat well. Add raisins.

Bake in a greased 8" tube pan at 350 degrees for 45 to 55 minutes.

Brush the top with a little butter and garnish with overlapping slices of crystallized ginger.

EDITH ROOSEVELT'S
FAT RASCALS (BISCUITS)

Theodore Roosevelt

- 2 cups flour, sifted
- 2 tablespoons sugar
- 2 teaspoons baking powder
- ½ teaspoon salt
- ¾ cup butter or margarine
- ½ pound dried currants
- ½ cup milk (about)

Thoroughly mix the flour, sugar, baking powder, and salt in a bowl. Cut in butter with a pastry blender or two knives until particles are the size of rice kernels.

Stir in currants. Add the milk and stir with a fork only until a soft dough is formed.

Shape dough lightly into a ball and roll out ½" thick on a lightly floured surface. Cut into rounds with a 2" cutter. Place on an ungreased baking sheet.

Bake at 450 degrees for 12 to 15 minutes.

Makes 1½ dozen.

PUMPKIN PIE

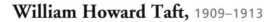

William Howard Taft, 1909–1913

> Crisco pastry for a single 9" pie crust
> ¼ cup granulated sugar
> ½ cup brown sugar
> ½ teaspoon salt
> ¼ teaspoon allspice
> 1 teaspoon cinnamon
> ½ teaspoon ginger (optional)
> 1½ cups pumpkin
> 2 eggs, separated
> ¾ cup canned milk
> ¾ cup fresh milk

Line a 9" pie pan with pastry. Mix sugars, salt, and spices. Add pumpkin. Add egg yolks and both canned and fresh milk. Add more spices, if desired. Last, fold in beaten egg whites, not too stiff. Pour filling into unbaked pie shell.

Bake at 450 degrees for 10 minutes, then turn down to 350 degrees until done, about 30 to 40 minutes (depending on your oven). The pie is ready when a knife comes out of filling clean.

TEA CAKES

★

Woodrow Wilson, 1913–1921

½ stick butter, softened
2 cups brown sugar
5 eggs
1 teaspoon baking soda
1 teaspoon nutmeg, freshly grated
1 teaspoon salt
8 cups flour
   Sugar, for dusting

Preheat oven to 375 degrees. In a large bowl, cream butter and sugar together until well blended. Beat in eggs, baking soda, nutmeg, and salt. Stir in flour and blend until dough is smooth.

Chill dough 4 hours.

Roll out dough to about ¼" thickness. Cut with 3" cookie cutters. Sprinkle with sugar. Bake on a cookie sheet (greased or lined with parchment or nonstick foil) for about 8 minutes.

Makes 6 dozen.

FILET MIGNON

Warren Harding, 1921–1923

4	pounds fillet
1½	cup sherry wine
2	lemons, juiced
	Salt and pepper
6	bacon strips
3	tablespoons butter
1½	pounds fresh mushrooms
2	tablespoons flour
2	tablespoons butter
1	cup beef stock
1½	teaspoons sherry wine
2	tablespoons lemon juice
6	sweet potatoes, baked and stuffed
1	can of asparagus tips
15	strips of red pepper for garnish

Marinate the filet with sherry wine and lemon juice; then season with salt and pepper. Place several long slices of bacon across the top, and stick toothpicks into the strips to hold them in place. Broil quickly at high heat for 8 minutes; then broil slowly for 5 minutes.

Cover with 3 tablespoons of butter.

Wash the mushrooms thoroughly, and remove the stems and skin. Add flour, butter and the stock; cook until tender, adding 1½ teaspoons sherry wine and a little lemon juice. Serve the mushrooms, whole, around the filet. Serve with stuffed sweet potatoes and green asparagus tips; garnish with strips of red pepper.

FLORENCE HARDING'S ALMOND COOKIES

★

Warren Harding

1 cup flour, sifted
⅓ cup sugar
⅓ cup blanched almonds, grated
⅓ cup soft butter
 Rind of 1 lemon, grated
2 eggs
 Pinch of salt
 Blanched almonds, for garnish

Sift flour and reserve. Mix sugar, grated almonds, butter, lemon rind, 1 whole egg, and salt together thoroughly with wooden spoon. Gradually work in the sifted flour.

Form the dough into a ball; wrap in wax paper, and chill for at least 1 hour.

Preheat oven to 350 degrees. Roll out the dough ¼" thick on a lightly floured board, and with cookie cutters, cut into cookies of desired sizes and shapes.

Place on greased baking sheet; brush with the other egg, which has been beaten; decorate each cookie with 3 blanched almonds.

Bake cookies for about 15 minutes, or until light brown.

ICE BOX COOKIES

Calvin Coolidge, 1923–1929

1	cup butter or shortening
2	cups brown sugar
3½	cups flour
1	teaspoon baking soda
½	teaspoon salt
1	cup walnut meats
2	eggs, well beaten

Cream the butter and sugar. Sift the flour, soda, and salt 3 times. Add nuts, eggs, and flour mixture. Mix all thoroughly, then pack into a long narrow bread pan and place in refrigerator overnight. The next day, unmold, slice very thin, and bake in a moderately hot oven. Do not grease the mold or baking pan.

If these cookies are baked at 375 degrees for 10 minutes, they will be nice and moist and chewy. Bake them a little longer if you want them crispy.

Makes 48 cookies.

CREAM PEACH PIE

Herbert Hoover, 1929–1933

2 to 3	fresh peaches
¾	cup cream
2	heaping tablespoons flour
⅔ to ¾	cup sugar
½	teaspoon vanilla
8"	unbaked pie shell

Slice peaches into 8" unbaked pie shell. Beat together cream and flour with sugar and vanilla. Pour over peaches. Bake at 400 degrees for 20 to 30 minutes.

> This recipe comes from Peg Anderson, whose grandmother was married to George Hoover, first cousin to Herbert Hoover. Peg is a park ranger at Herbert Hoover National Historic Site.

GIRL SCOUT COOKIES

Herbert Hoover

1	cup butter or margarine
1	cup sugar
2	eggs
2	tablespoons milk
1	teaspoon vanilla
1	teaspoon salt
2½	cups flour
1	teaspoon baking powder

Cream butter and sugar. Add well beaten eggs, then milk, vanilla, salt, flour, and baking powder.

Chill. Roll thinly, cut out, and bake at 350 degrees on a greased cookie sheet for about 8 minutes, or until golden brown. Sprinkle sugar on top.

Makes 6 to 7 dozen cookies.

FRANKLIN ROOSEVELT'S BIRTHDAY CAKE

Franklin D. Roosevelt, 1933–1945

1	cup butter or margarine
1½	cups sugar
3	eggs, well beaten
2	cups flour
½	teaspoon salt
1	teaspoon baking soda
½	cup cocoa
1	cup cold black coffee
1	tablespoon vinegar
½	teaspoon vanilla

Cream butter and add sugar, a little at a time. Cream well; add eggs. Sift flour, salt, soda, and cocoa together 3 times. Add coffee with flour mixture to batter, alternating.

Then add vinegar and vanilla. Bake at 350 degrees in a 9" greased layer pan for 20 to 35 minutes or in a loaf pan for about 30 to 40 minutes.

ELEANOR ROOSEVELT'S PECAN PIE

Franklin D. Roosevelt

CRUST

1½	cups flour
½	teaspoon salt
1	teaspoon baking powder
½	cup shortening
¼	cup ice water

FILLING

⅓	cup butter
1	cup brown sugar
3 or 4	eggs
1	cup light corn syrup
1	cup pecans, chopped
1	teaspoon vanilla
¼	teaspoon salt
	Whole pecans, for garnish
	1 pint cream, whipped, for garnish

CRUST

Measure 1½ cups flour; sift with salt and baking powder. Divide shortening into two equal parts. Cut half into the flour mixture until it looks like corn meal. Cut the remaining half of the shortening coarsely until the size of large green peas. Over the mixture, sprinkle 3 tablespoons ice water. Blend lightly.

If the dough holds together, add no more liquid; if not, add additional water. Line pie pan with crust.

FILLING

Cream ⅓ cup butter with 1 cup brown sugar. Beat in eggs, one at a time; stir in 1 cup light corn syrup, 1 cup coarsely chopped pecans, 1 teaspoon vanilla and ¼ teaspoon salt.

(continued)

Fill the pie shell with the mixture. Preheat oven to 375 degrees and bake the pie for about 35 to 40 minutes.

When the pie is set and has cooled off, decorate the top with pecan halves. Garnish with whipped cream around the entire edge. The whipped cream may be further trimmed with any leftover small pieces of pie crust dough.

BESS TRUMAN'S
OZARK PUDDING

Harry S. Truman, 1945–1953

    1   egg
    ¾   cup sugar
    2   tablespoons all-purpose flour
  1¼   teaspoon baking powder
    ¼   teaspoon salt
    ½   cup peeled apples, chopped
    ½   cup nuts, chopped
    1   teaspoon vanilla
        Whipped cream (with a touch of rum, if desired)
        or vanilla ice cream

Preheat the oven to 350 degrees. Grease a 10" greased pie pan.

Beat the egg and sugar together until smooth. Add the flour, baking powder, and salt. Blend well. Fold in the apples, nuts, and vanilla.

Pour into the prepared pie pan and bake for 30 to 35 minutes. Remove from the oven; the pudding will fall, but it is supposed to. Serve warm with whipped cream or ice cream.

Makes 6 servings.

MAMIE EISENHOWER'S PUMPKIN PIE

Dwight D. Eisenhower, 1953–1961

2 envelopes unflavored gelatin

1½ cups light brown sugar, firmly packed

1 teaspoon salt

3 teaspoons pumpkin pie spice

¾ cup milk

6 eggs, separated

14 ounces canned pumpkin

½ cup granulated sugar

2 graham cracker pie crust shells

Cool Whip or whipped cream for topping

In a 3 quart metal mixing bowl, thoroughly stir together gelatin, brown sugar, salt, and pumpkin pie spice; stir in milk. With a whisk, beat in egg yolks, then pumpkin.

Place bowl over a saucepan of boiling water: cook, stirring often, until heated through and gelatin and sugar have dissolved, about 10 to 15 min. (Test by feel; if it's too hot to touch then it's cooked). Chill until mixture mounds when dropped from a spoon.

Beat egg whites into soft peaks; gradually beat in granulated sugar until stiff, then fold into gelatin mixture. Turn into pie shells; chill until firm. Before serving, top with whipped cream or Cool Whip.

Makes two 9" pies.

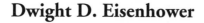

Dwight D. Eisenhower

4½ cups sugar
    Pinch salt
2   tablespoons butter
1   (12-ounce) can evaporated milk
2   cups coarsely chopped pecans
1   pint (1 jar) marshmallow cream
12 ounces semisweet chocolate
12 ounces German sweet chocolate

In a heavy saucepan over medium heat, bring the sugar, salt, butter, and evaporated milk to a boil. Boil for 6 minutes.

Meanwhile, place the pecans, marshmallow cream, and chocolate in a large bowl. Pour the boiled syrup over the chocolate mixture. Beat until chocolate is all melted.

Spray a 15½ × 10½ × 1" jelly-roll pan with a nonstick cooking spray and pour fudge into pan. Let harden at room temperature before cutting into 1 squares (can be placed in the refrigerator or freezer to speed hardening process).

Makes 4 pounds.

When Mamie Eisenhower came to the White House, she brought along a recipe for fudge that called for marshmallow crème. Her candy was so creamy the president reportedly called it the "million dollar" fudge.

PUREE MONGOL SOUP

John F. Kennedy, 1961–1963

1 can condensed pea soup

1 can condensed tomato soup

1 can milk

1 can water

   Dash of curry powder

Mix ingredients, then heat and serve.

Makes 4 servings.

This was FBI Director J. Edgar Hoover's favorite soup. Ironically, this was also a favorite in the John F. Kennedy White House—not for the faint of heart.

JACKIE KENNEDY'S WHITE HOUSE HOT FRUIT DESSERT

John F. Kennedy

1	orange
1	lemon
½	cup light brown sugar, packed
¼	teaspoon ground nutmeg
8¾	ounces (1 can) pineapple tidbits
8	ounces (1 can) apricots
8¾	ounces (1 can) peaches
17	ounces (1 can) pitted bing cherries
16	ounces sour cream
1	jarred prune (optional)

Grate the rind of the orange and lemon and add to the light brown sugar and nutmeg.

Cut orange and lemon into very thin slices.

Drain and combine fruits.

Butter a 1-quart casserole and arrange layers of drained canned fruits and lemon and orange slices, sprinkled with light brown sugar; repeat.

Bake at 350 for 30 minutes.

Serve warm with a dollop of sour cream on top.

Makes 6 to 8 servings.

Delicious baked fruit for breakfast, brunch, or an elegant dessert

SPICE TEA

Lyndon B. Johnson, 1963–1969

6   teaspoons loose tea (or 8 teabags)
2   cups boiling water
1   small can frozen lemon juice
1   small can frozen orange juice
1½   cups sugar
2   quarts water
1   cinnamon stick

Pour water over tea and let cool. Strain into a large saucepan and add remaining ingredients. Simmer for 20 minutes. If too strong, add water. Add extra sugar to taste.

Remove cinnamon stick before serving.

Makes 16 to 20 cups.

> This recipe was one of Mrs. Johnson's favorites. She served it to guests at the ranch or the White House on chilly days.

SHRIMP CURRY À LA ZEPHYR WRIGHT

★

Lyndon B. Johnson

2 pounds raw shrimp, shelled and deveined
5 tablespoons butter
½ cup onions, minced
6 tablespoons flour
2½ teaspoons curry powder
1¼ teaspoons salt
1 teaspoon sugar
½ teaspoon powdered ginger
1 chicken bouillon cube, dissolved in 1 cup boiling water
2 cups milk
1 teaspoon lemon juice

Steam shrimp until done, approximately 5 minutes or until pink.

Sauté onions in melted butter until tender.

Stir in flour, curry powder, salt, sugar, and ginger.

Dissolve bouillon cube in water.

Gradually combine bouillon and milk with onion and spice mixture, stirring until thickened.

Add cooked shrimp and lemon juice, cooking only enough to heat through.

Serve over rice.

Makes 8 servings.

(continued)

Zephyr Wright was both maid and cook for President Lyndon Johnson. Leonard H. Marks, director of the U.S. Information Agency during the Johnson administration, tells this story about how she may have influenced his work on civil rights reform:

> Many say that Lyndon, because he came from the South, didn't believe in civil rights. Lady Bird had two people as hired help, Zephyr and Sammy Wright. Zephyr was the maid and cook, and Sammy was the chauffeur. At one of the luncheons I attended before Johnson became president, Zephyr was serving when Lyndon told her that she and Sammy should get ready to drive to Austin. The family would join them later. She said, "Senator, I'm not going to do it." There was silence.
>
> She said, "When Sammy and I drive to Texas and I have to go to the bathroom, like Lady Bird or the girls, I am not allowed to go to the bathroom. I have to find a bush and squat. When it comes time to eat, we can't go into restaurants. We have to eat out of a brown bag. And at night, Sammy sleeps in the front of the car with the steering wheel around his neck, while I sleep in the back. We are not going to do it again."
>
> LBJ put down his napkin and walked out of the room. Later, when Johnson became president and signed the Civil Rights Act of 1964 into law, Zephyr was there. Johnson motioned to her, gave her the pen that he used to sign the bill. He said, "You deserve this more than anybody else."

Source: LBJ Library.

LBJ'S FAVORITE CHILI

★

Lyndon B. Johnson

4 pounds coarsely ground beef (chili-grind)
1 large onion, chopped
2 cloves garlic, minced
1 teaspoon dried oregano
1 teaspoon ground cumin
6 teaspoons chili powder
32 ounces (2 cans) tomatoes
2 cups hot water
   Salt to taste

In a large frying pan, brown meat with onion and garlic until meat is lightly browned; transfer ingredients to a large kettle.

Add oregano, cumin, chili powder, tomatoes, salt, and hot water.

Bring just to a boil; lower heat and simmer, covered, for approximately 1 hour. Remove from heat.

Skim off grease and serve.

Makes 12 servings.

LBJ'S PICKLED OKRA

Lyndon B. Johnson

3   pounds whole okra

6   hot peppers

6   cloves garlic, peeled

2   teaspoons apple cider vinegar

½   cup salt

1   tablespoon mustard seed

Wash and scrub okra and pack in clean jars. Add to each jar 1 hot pepper and 1 clove garlic. Boil remaining ingredients. Cover okra with hot liquid, filling to within ½" of the jar lid. Adjust lids. Process in boiling water for 10 minutes.

LADYBIRD JOHNSON'S LEMON CAKE

★

Lyndon B. Johnson

CAKE

¾	cup butter or margarine, room temperature
1¼	cups granulated sugar
8	egg yolks
2½	cups cake flour
3	teaspoons baking powder
¼	teaspoon salt
¾	cup milk
1	teaspoon vanilla extract
1	teaspoon lemon rind, grated
1	teaspoon lemon juice

LEMON ICING

2	cups confectioners' sugar
¼	cup butter or margarine, room temperature
1	lemon, grated rind only
1	lemon, juiced
2	teaspoons cream (or more, for spreading consistency)
	Yellow food coloring (optional)

CAKE

Cream butter and sugar until fluffy. In a separate bowl, beat egg yolks until light and lemon colored; blend into creamed mixture. Sift together flour, baking powder, and salt; resift 3 times. Add s¨ ingredients to creamed mixture in thirds, alternating with milk the batter thoroughly after each addition.

Add vanilla extract, lemon rind, and lemon juice; beat fc 2 minutes. Bake in greased muffin pan in a preheated oven

(*continued*)

325 degrees for 30 minutes or until cake tester inserted in center comes out clean. You can also use three 9" round cake pans and bake at 350 degrees for 25 minutes or a Bundt pan and bake for 1 hour at 325 degrees. Double the frosting recipe for a layer cake.

LEMON ICING

Combine ingredients and beat, adding cream until desired consistency is reached.

Behind every great president is a great first lady, and behind at least one first lady—Ladybird Johnson—was a great arsenal of awesome cake recipes. We went for one of her (and the president's) favorites, taking a modern twist and making it into cupcakes—cupcakes that are light, fluffy, and simply delicious, so refreshing that they provide a nice foil to all of those other holiday foods!

PAT NIXON'S MEATLOAF

Richard Nixon, 1969–1974

2	tablespoons butter
1	cup onions, finely chopped
2	garlic cloves, minced
3	slices white bead
1	cup milk
2	pounds lean ground beef
2	eggs, lightly beaten
1	teaspoon salt
1	tablespoon fresh parsley , chopped
½	teaspoon dried thyme
½	teaspoon dried marjoram
2	tablespoons tomato puree
2	tablespoons bread crumbs
	Ground black pepper to taste

Grease a 9" × 13" baking pan. Melt butter in a sauté pan. Add onions and garlic and sauté until just golden; do not brown. Let cool.

Dice bread and soak it in milk. In a large mixing bowl, mix ground beef by hand with sautéed onions, garlic, and bread pieces.

Add eggs, salt, pepper, parsley, thyme, and marjoram and mix by hand in a circular motion.

Turn this mixture into the prepared baking pan and pat into a loaf shape, leaving at least 1" of space around the edges to allow fat to run off. Brush the top with the tomato puree and sprinkle with bread crumbs.

Refrigerate for 1 hour to allow the flavors to penetrate and to firm up the loaf.

Preheat the oven to 375 degrees.

Bake the meatloaf on the lower shelf of the oven for 1 hour, or until the meat is cooked through. Pour off accumulated fat several times while baking and after the meat is fully cooked. Let stand on a wire rack for 5 minutes before slicing.

NIXON'S BAKED GRAPEFRUIT

Richard Nixon

1   large grapefruit
1   teaspoon honey
1   tablespoon brown sugar
1   large strawberry
2 or 3   fresh mint leaves
     Powdered sugar

Slice off the top third of the grapefruit. Remove the center core and separate sections with a serrated knife for easy eating.

Spread the surface of the grapefruit with honey and sprinkle with sugar. Place under a broiler, turning to heat evenly until glaze is bubbly, for 5 minutes.

Garnish the center with a fresh strawberry and mint leaves. Dust with powdered sugar and serve at once. To serve as a dessert, add a teaspoon of dark rum to the honey.

Makes 2 servings.

RUBY-RED GRAPEFRUIT CHICKEN

★

Gerald Ford, 1974–1977

2 ruby-red grapefruits
½ cup whole cranberry sauce
1 tablespoon honey
¼ teaspoon cloves
¼ teaspoon salt
1 fryer, disjointed
3 tablespoons butter or margarine

Peel and section the grapefruits, squeezing all juice from the membranes into a saucepan. Add cranberry sauce, honey, cloves, and salt, mixing well; then bring to a boil. Stir in grapefruit sections.

Brown chicken in butter in a frying pan, then place in a shallow baking dish. Baste with the grapefruit sauce.

Bake at 350 degrees for about 45 minutes, basting frequently. Serve chicken with the remaining grapefruit sauce.

Makes 4 servings.

BETTY FORD'S BLUEBERRY BANANA BREAD

★

Gerald Ford

2   cups sugar
2   sticks butter
2   teaspoons vanilla
4   eggs
5   medium bananas, mashed
4   cups flour, divided
3   tablespoons baking soda
1   teaspoon baking powder
½   teaspoon salt
2   cups blueberries

Preheat oven to 325 degrees. Grease and flour 2 loaf pans. Cream together butter and sugar; add vanilla. Beat in eggs; add bananas, then 2 cups of flour.

Measure 2 cups flour, reserving 2 tablespoons to coat the blueberries. Place the flour in a sifter with the remaining dry ingredients. Sift and fold into the banana mixture. Sprinkle 2 tablespoons of flour over the blueberries and coat well, then fold into the batter. Divide the batter into the prepared loaf pans.

Bake for approximately 50 minutes.

Makes 2 loaves.

PEANUT BRITTLE

Jimmy Carter, 1977–1981

    2   cups sugar
    1   cup corn syrup, clear
   ½   cup water
    1   cup butter
    4   cups peanuts, raw
    1   teaspoon baking soda

Blend sugar, corn syrup, water, and butter.

Cook to 230 degrees as measured by a candy thermometer.

Add peanuts and cook to 280 degrees. Stir occasionally and continue cooking to 305 degrees.

Remove from heat.

Add baking soda and stir quickly until mixture foams.

Quickly pour into 2 buttered 15" × 10" × 1" pans and spread thinly over entire surface.

Cool until hard and break into pieces.

SUCCOTASH WITH SAUSAGE

Jimmy Carter

1	pound sausage links
2	tablespoons butter
½	cup onions, finely chopped
3	large ripe tomatoes, peeled and seeded
2	cups fresh or frozen lima beans
1½	cups fresh or frozen corn kernels
1	cup tomato juice
1½	teaspoons salt
¼	teaspoon freshly ground white pepper
1	tablespoon parsley, chopped

In a large skillet, cook sausages over medium high heat until they are cooked thoroughly. Brown for 10 minutes. Drain fat, cover, and keep warm.

In a separate skillet, melt butter and sauté onions over medium heat for 3 minutes or until transparent. Do not brown.

Dice tomatoes and add to sautéed onions. Stir in lima beans, corn, tomato juice, salt, and pepper.

Cover and simmer for 25 minutes. Stir occasionally.

Transfer to a deep serving dish. Arrange sausage links across the top.

Sprinkle with chopped parsley and serve immediately.

Makes 4 servings.

PECAN TOFFEE TASSIES

Jimmy Carter

15	ounces (1 package) refrigerated pie crusts
¼	cup (½ stick) butter, melted
1	cup brown sugar, firmly packed
2	tablespoons all-purpose flour
2	large eggs, lightly beaten
1	teaspoon vanilla extract
1	cup pecans, finely chopped
10	ounces (1 package) almond brickle chips

Preheat the oven to 350 degrees.

Unroll the pie crusts onto a lightly floured surface. Roll into two 15" circles. Cut out 48 circles using a 1¾" fluted or round cookie cutter, rerolling the dough as needed. Place in 1¾" muffin pans, pressing on the bottoms and up the sides of each of the minimuffin cups. Combine the melted butter, brown sugar, flour, and eggs in a large bowl, mixing well. Add the vanilla. Stir in the pecans and brickle chips. Spoon the pecan filling evenly into the pie shells. Bake for 25 minutes, or until the filling is set and the crust is lightly browned. Cool in pans on wire racks.

> Now, Jimmy Carter did have holiday meals at the White House, but even more importantly, he was the first presidential figure ever to bake with Paula Deen—so you could say that these cookies are a step above. The Carters served these at Christmas parties. They were stickier and less pretty than Paula's, but, were they ever rich and delicious!

NANCY REAGAN'S
MONKEY BREAD

Ronald Regan, 1981–1989

1	package dry yeast
1 to 1¼	cups milk
3	eggs
3	tablespoons sugar
1	teaspoon salt
4½	cups flour
6	ounces butter, room temperature, plus ½ pound, melted
1	9" ring mold

In a bowl, mix yeast with a small amount of milk until dissolved. Add 2 eggs and beat. Mix in dry ingredients. Add the remaining milk a little at a time, mixing thoroughly. Cut in butter until it is blended. Knead dough, then let it rise for 1 to 1 ½ hours until double in size.

Roll dough onto a floured board and shape into a log. Cut log into 24 pieces of equal size. Shape each piece of dough into a ball and roll in melted butter.

Place 12 balls in the bottom of the buttered and floured mold, leaving space between them. Place the remaining balls on top, spacing evenly.

Let dough rise in mold for 30 minutes.

Brush the top with the remaining egg. Bake in a preheated oven at 375 degrees until golden brown, approximately 25 to 30 minutes.

The former first lady created a winner with this one.

THE REAGAN FAMILY CRANBERRY SAUCE

★

Ronald Reagan

3   teaspoons orange juice concentrate
⅔   cup water
½   teaspoon dry mustard
3⅓   cups sugar
3   cups cranberries

Mix orange juice, water, dry mustard, and sugar in a large sauce pan. Add the cranberries and heat until they all pop. Serve and enjoy.

> Dry mustard is the secret ingredient in this Thanksgiving family favorite.

NANCY REAGAN'S PERSIMMON PUDDING

Ronald Reagan

½ cup butter, melted
1 cup sugar
1 cup flour, sifted
¼ teaspoon salt
1 teaspoon ground cinnamon
¼ teaspoon nutmeg
2 teaspoons baking soda
1 cup persimmon pulp (ripe ones)
2 teaspoons warm water
3 tablespoons brandy, plus extra for flambéing
1 teaspoon vanilla
2 eggs, slightly beaten
1 cup seedless raisins

Stir together the melted butter and sugar. Sift the flour with salt, cinnamon, nutmeg, and baking soda, and add to the butter and sugar mixture. Add the persimmon pulp until it dissolves in a warm mixture of water, brandy, and vanilla. Add the eggs, mixing thoroughly but lightly. Add the raisins and nuts. Put the mixture in a buttered steam-type covered mold and steam for 2½ hours. Flambé at the table with brandy.

BRANDY WHIPPED CREAM SAUCE

★

Ronald Reagan

    1   egg
   ⅓   cup melted butter
    1   cup powdered sugar, sifted
    1   tablespoon brandy flavoring
        Dash of salt
    1   cup whipping cream

Beat the egg until light and fluffy. Beat in the butter, powdered sugar, brandy flavoring, and salt. Beat the cream until it is stiff. Gently fold it into the first mixture. Cover and chill until ready to serve. Stir before spooning on the Persimmon Pudding.

What Ronald and Nancy Reagan brought to Washington was, in a word, polish. They infused California chic in a southern town that often plays poorer second cousin to New York or Los Angeles. At formal state dinners and glamorous entertaining at the White House, especially around the winter holidays—should you have been so lucky as to have your presence requested at 1600 Pennsylvania Avenue—you would surely have been served some of the former first lady's elegant Persimmon Pudding with Brandy Whipped Cream Sauce and perhaps a slice or two of Monkey Bread.

RONALD REAGAN'S HAMBURGER SOUP

★

Ronald Reagan

    2   pounds lean ground beef
    2   tablespoons butter
    2   cups onions, diced
    2   cloves garlic, chopped
1½   cups carrots, sliced
    2   cups celery, sliced
    1   cup green peppers, diced
    3   quarts (12 cups) beef broth or water with bouillon cubes
  16 ounces tomato, canned or fresh, chopped
  ¼   teaspoon ground black pepper
  10 ounces (canned) hominy

Brown meat in butter in a 6-quart sauce pan. Add onions, garlic, carrots, celery, and green peppers. Simmer for 10 minutes with the pan covered.

Add beef broth or water with bouillon cubes. Add chopped tomato and ground pepper. Simmer soup on low heat for 35 minutes. Add hominy. Boil hamburger soup for 10 minutes more.

Makes 4 quarts.

There's been speculation that this first made news after President Reagan innocently announced his liking for fancy French soups . . . and was immediately accused of being elitist. Nevertheless, it is definitely a homespun, plain soup and not as bad as you might think when you see that there is hominy in it. This corn product—with an Algonquin Native American name—was an important food to early U.S. pioneers. It is a nice, firm little ball in the soup—almost dumplinglike.

Serve the soup as a lunch meal for 4 to 6 people with lots of cornbread, cold milk, and maybe a big American pie for dessert. We give the recipe verbatim—note the nonelitist allowance for canned foods and bouillon cubes.

REAGAN'S FAVORITE MACARONI AND CHEESE

Ronald Reagan

½   pound macaroni
1   tablespoon butter
1   egg, beaten
1   teaspoon dry mustard
1   teaspoon salt
1   teaspoon Worcestershire sauce
3   cups sharp cheddar cheese, grated, reserving some
    for topping
1   cup warm milk
    Pinch paparika

Boil macaroni in water until tender and drain thoroughly. Stir in butter and egg.

Mix mustard and salt with Worcestershire sauce and add to milk.

Add cheese, leaving enough to sprinkle on top.

Pour into buttered casserole; add milk and sprinkle with cheese. Add paprika.

Bake at 350 degrees for about 45 minutes or until custard is set and top is crusty.

Makes 4 entrees or 6 to 8 side dishes.

PUMPKIN PECAN PIE

Ronald Reagan

    4   eggs, slightly beaten
    2   cups canned or mashed cooked pumpkin
    1   cup granulated sugar
    ½   cup dark corn syrup
    1   teaspoon vanilla extract
    ½   teaspoon ground cinnamon
    ¼   teaspoon salt
    1   9" pastry shell. unbaked
    1   cup pecans, chopped

Combine all ingredients, except pecans. Pour into pie shell. Top with pecans.

Bake in preheated 350 degree oven for 40 minutes, or until set.

BARBARA BUSH'S LEMON BARS

George H. W. Bush, 1989–1993

CRUST

1   cup margarine

2   cups powdered sugar

2   cups flour

FILLING

4   teaspoons lemon juice

2   lemon rinds, grated

4   eggs, well beaten

2   cups sugar

1   teaspoon baking powder

4   tablespoons flour

1   cup coconut, shredded

CRUST

Mix the margarine, powdered sugar, and flour.

Spread in a 15" × 10" jelly roll pan.

Bake at 350 degrees for 15 minutes until pale tan. Cool.

FILLING

Mix the filling ingredients and pour over the crust.

Bake for 25 minutes at 350 degrees. Cut into bars.

Makes 24 bars.

MUSHROOM QUICHE

George H. W. Bush

1	9" pie crust, unbaked
3	tablespoons unsalted butter
1¼	pounds mushrooms, sliced
3	green onions, minced
1	garlic clove, minced
3	shallots, minced
1¾	teaspoons oregano
1¾	teaspoons basil
1¼	teaspoons salt
¾	teaspoon marjoram
¼	teaspoon black pepper
¼	teaspoon thyme
½	teaspoon dry mustard
4	eggs
¾	cup skim or whole milk or half-and-half

Position rack in lower ⅓ of oven and preheat to 375 degrees. Melt butter in large skillet over medium high heat. Sauté the mushrooms, onions, garlic, and shallots together.

Stir in seasonings and cook 2 minutes until liquid is evaporated. Let cook 5 minutes. In a medium bowl combine eggs with milk or cream and heat well. Stir in mushroom mixture and pour into pie crust.

Bake until filling is puffed, set, and starting to begin to turn brown—about 35 to 45 minutes.

BARBARA BUSH'S CHOCOLATE CHIP COOKIES

★

George H. W. Bush

½	cup butter, softened
⅓	cup brown sugar, packed
⅓	cup white granulated sugar
1	egg
1½	teaspoons hot water
½	teaspoon vanilla extract
1⅛	cups all-purpose flour
½	teaspoon baking soda
½	teaspoon salt
1	cup semisweet chocolate chips

Beat butter, brown sugar, white granulated sugar, and egg until light and fluffy, about 3 minutes. Beat in hot water and vanilla. Gradually beat in flour, baking soda, and salt, until well blended and smooth. Stir in chocolate chips.

Drop the dough by well-rounded teaspoons onto greased cookie sheets.

Bake at 375 degrees for 10 minutes, or until golden.

Cool the cookie sheet on a wire rack for 1 minute, then remove cookies to a rack to cool completely.

Makes 3 dozen.

BARBARA BUSH'S VEGETABLE SALAD

★

George H. W. Bush

SALAD

2	pounds fresh spinach, chopped
10	hard-boiled eggs, sliced
1	pound bacon, cooked and crumbled
1	medium head lettuce, shredded
1	cup shallots, sliced
10	ounces thawed frozen peas, uncooked

SALAD DRESSING

½	cup mayonnaise
2½	cups sour cream
½	cup Swiss cheese, grated, for topping
	Worcestershire sauce to taste
	Lemon juice to taste
	Salt and pepper

SALAD

Place ingredients in order in a large salad bowl.

SALAD DRESSING

Blend dressing ingredients, except cheese, together and pour over salad. Top with Swiss cheese. Cover and chill for 12 hours. Do not toss until serving time.

Makes 12 servings.

CHOCOLATE CHIP COOKIES

William Jefferson Clinton, 1993–2001

- 1½ cups flour
- 1 teaspoon salt
- 1 teaspoon baking soda
- 1 cup shortening
- 1 cup brown sugar, packed
- ½ cup white sugar
- 1 teaspoon vanilla extract
- 2 eggs
- 2 cups rolled oats
- 2 cups semisweet chocolate chips

Preheat the oven to 350 degrees. Brush baking sheets lightly with vegetable oil or spray with a cooking spray.

Combine flour, salt, and baking soda on waxed paper.

Beat together shortening, brown sugar, white sugar, and vanilla extract in a large bowl with an electric mixer until creamy. Add eggs and beat until light and fluffy.

Gradually beat in flour mixture. Stir in rolled oats and then semisweet chocolate chips.

Drop batter by rounded teaspoonfuls onto greased baking sheets. Bake for 8 to 10 minutes, or until golden brown.

Cool the cookies on sheets for 2 minutes. Place the cookies on wire racks to cool completely.

Makes 7 dozen.

According to the lore surrounding these cookies, Hillary used to make them for congressmen and other politicos when she was Arkansas's first lady. I hear Bill liked them too.

FAVORITE CHICKEN ENCHILADAS

William Jefferson Clinton

12 ounces broccoli

2 teaspoons olive oil

1 medium red onion, finely chopped

2 medium cloves garlic, minced

½ jalapeno pepper, minced

1 teaspoon ground cumin

½ teaspoon chili powder

¼ teaspoon ground cinnamon

8 ounces skinless, boneless chicken breast, cooked and shredded

15 ounces (1 can) no-salt-added whole tomatoes

2 tablespoons fresh cilantro, minced

½ cup evaporated skim milk

6 small corn tortillas

¾ cup reduced-fat Monterey Jack cheese, shredded

2 cups brown rice, cooked

1 cup nonfat yogurt

¼ teaspoon salt (optional)

Preheat oven to 350 degrees. Remove tough stems from the broccoli and break into florets. Steam broccoli until crisp but tender and set aside.

In a large nonstick pan, heat oil; sauté onion for 3 or 4 minutes to soften.

Add garlic, jalapeno, cumin, chili powder, cinnamon, and chicken. Stir and cook to mix well and heat through. Season with salt, if desired. Remove from the heat and stir in broccoli; divide into 6 equal portions and set aside.

In a blender or food processor, combine tomatoes, cilantro, and evaporated milk; blend well. Pour mixture into a pot and heat just to boiling. Remove from heat and dip each tortilla into the hot mixture to soften slightly. Fill each tortilla with ⅙ of the chicken mixture; roll up and place seam side down in a baking dish large enough to hold all the enchiladas in a single layer. Repeat the process for all tortillas and pour the remaining tomato-milk mixture over the enchiladas; sprinkle cheese over the top. Bake 15 to 20 minutes, or until the sauce is bubbly, and serve with brown rice and a dollop of yogurt.

CARROT MUFFINS

George W. Bush, 2001–2009

1	cup all-purpose flour
1	teaspoon baking soda
½	teaspoon ground cinnamon
2	eggs, room temperature
¾	cup canola or sunflower oil
1	teaspoon vanilla
1	cup sugar
1½	cup carrots, shredded
½	cup pecans, coarsely chopped

Preheat oven to 350 degrees. Line 12 muffin molds with paper cup liners. Combine flour, baking soda, and cinnamon in a medium bowl.

Place the eggs, oil, vanilla, and sugar together in a mixing bowl. Whisk for about 5 minutes.

Stir in flour mixture until combined. Stir in carrots and pecans. Fill cups to ¾ full.

Bake until a toothpick inserted into the center of a muffin comes out clean, approximately 18 to 20 minutes.

Cool in a pan for about 5 minutes and invert the muffins onto a rack.

Makes 1 dozen.

WHITE HOUSE EGGNOG

★

George W. Bush

5   ounces egg yolks (6 to 7 yolks)
1   cup sugar
¾   cup bourbon
¾   cup cognac
¾   cup dark rum
7   ounces egg whites (6 to 7 eggs)
1   teaspoon salt
2   cups heavy cream
1   tablespoon pure vanilla extract
1   quart milk, plus more if needed
    Nutmeg, for garnish

Put the yolks and sugar in the bowl of a standing mixer fitted with the whisk attachment; whip until pale yellow ribbons form, 5 to 7 minutes.

Add the bourbon, cognac, and rum; whip well, scrape down the sides, and mix again. Transfer the mixture to a 6-quart bowl.

In a separate, clean mixer bowl, whip the egg whites and salt until very stiff peaks form. Fold into the eggnog mixture.

Wipe out the mixer bowl, pour in the cream and vanilla, and whip until very stiff peaks form. Fold this into the eggnog mixture. Add the milk and whisk until smooth, 3 to 5 minutes.

Chill, garnish with nutmeg (and cinnamon), and enjoy!

(continued)

For 11 years spanning the William J. Clinton and George W. Bush presidencies, this eggnog recipe has ruled. In *White House Chef*, Walter Scheiber describes how "every year, the holiday season was kicked off with the 'running of the "nog",' a playful way of referring to the tour of the House we made with the eggnog (and a riff on the "running of the bulls" in Pamplona, Spain)."

What can we say? This is the real deal—it certainly packs a punch, and even if it was just Thanksgiving, it certainly put our crew in a celebratory mood.

LAURA BUSH'S HOT CHOCOLATE ★

George W. Bush

6	tablespoons unsweetened cocoa
6	tablespoons sugar
	Pinch of salt
2½	cups milk
2½	cups light cream
	Pinch of cinnamon powder (optional)
½	teaspoons (or more) vanilla
	Whipped cream
	Orange zest

Mix cocoa, salt, and sugar. Add milk.

Heat to dissolve.

Add light cream, cinnamon, and vanilla. Heat to just under boiling.

Mix very well and pour into warm mugs.

Top with whipped cream, cocoa powder, and fine orange zest.

Makes 6 servings.

> This is one of George and Laura Bush's favorite Christmas recipes.

MUSHROOM SOUP

George W. Bush

1	leek (white only), finely diced
1	small sweet onion, finely diced
½	pound wild mushrooms (chanterelle or yellow foot)
½	pound shiitake mushrooms
½	pound cremini mushrooms
2	garlic cloves, chopped
½	teaspoon fresh thyme, chopped
1	tablespoon flour
1½	quarts chicken stock
1	pint heavy cream
	Butter
	Salt and Pepper

Cook leek and onion over low heat in a small covered stock pot with a little butter. Do not allow to color.

Clean and chop all the mushrooms and add to the leek and onion mixture. Add chopped garlic and thyme. Continue to cook, adding more butter if necessary, until all the mushrooms are cooked.

Sprinkle in a level tablespoon of flour and mix well. Add 1 quart of chicken stock and bring to a simmer for 20 minutes. Keep stirring.

Add 1 cup of cream and cook for 5 more minutes.

Put the soup in a blender and puree. Leave it a little chunky and return it to the stove. Add salt and pepper, as well as more cream and the remainder of the chicken stock, if necessary.

Makes 6 servings.

THE OBAMA FAMILY'S LINGUINI

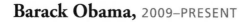

Barack Obama, 2009–PRESENT

1½   pounds fresh shrimp in their shells
3–4   garlic cloves
1   box linguini
1   tablespoon olive oil
    Salt and pepper to taste
½   cup sun-dried tomatoes, sliced in olive oil
2   cups chicken broth, hot
    Fresh basil, julienned

Clean and devein shrimp. Remove the shells and soak them in hot chicken broth.

Thinly slice garlic (the more garlic, the better the flavor of the dish).

Cook the pasta and set aside. (It is important not to over cook the pasta.)

In a large sauté pan, heat the olive oil on high heat and sauté the garlic cloves until they begin to brown slightly.

Add fresh shrimp and cook until it just begins to turn pink. Add salt and pepper to flavor shrimp. Add sun-dried tomatoes and continue to cook for another minute.

Mix the pasta into the garlic, shrimp, and sun-dried tomato mixture until the pasta is coated entirely. Add salt and pepper to taste.

Slowly add a bit of the shrimp shell and chicken broth liquid to remove the reserves from bottom of pan.

Remove the pan from the heat and let sit for a few moments.

Sprinkle basil over the top of the dish before serving.

Makes 4 servings.

Recipe Index

Favorite Dishes of the Presidents

Pumpkin Pecan Pie, 352
Pumpkin Pie, 317
Sam's Scrumptious Pie, 220–221
Sixth District Apple Pie, 241–242
Swish Pie, 218
Texas Pecan Chocolate Chip Pie, 232
Ulysses Grant's Lemon Pie, 300–301
Zoe's Pecan Pie, 214

Desserts

Abigail Adams's Apple Pan Dowdy, 272
Abigail Adams's Beggar's Pudding with Sack
    Sauce, 274
Ambrosia Fruit and Nut Mold, 236
Baked Apples, 240
Baklava, 225–226
Bess Truman's Ozark Pudding, 327
Blitz Kuchen, 213
Charlotte Russe, 285
Chocolate Chip Caramel Bars, 234
Chocolate Melt-Away Dessert, 228
Chocolate Mousse, 235
Congressman Peter King's Lemon Squares, 211
Cranberry Pudding, 266
Jackie Kennedy's White House Hot Fruit Dessert,
    331
Lemon Mousse, 227
Mamie Eisenhower's Fudge, 329
Michelle Obama's Apple Cobbler, 206–207
Minnesota Rhubarb Dessert, 245
Mom's English Scones, 210
Nancy Reagan's Persimmon Pudding, 348
Pumpkin Torte, 223–224
Rachel Jackson's Burnt Custard, 284
Rice Pudding with Lemon Sauce, 298–299
South Alabama Peanut Clusters, 209
Strawberry Ice Cream, 229
Thomas Jefferson's Bread Pudding, 276
Tyler Pudding, 287

Potpourri: Snacks, Sauces, and Drinks

Avocado Salsa, 147
Baked Fruit, 250
Brandy Whipped Cream Sauce, 349
Cranberry-Apple-Pear Sauce, 249
Dolly Madison's Fairy Butter, 279

French Mints, 251
George Washington's Beer, 271
George Washington's Eggnog, 259
Honey Mustard Dressing, 254
Laura Bush's Hot Chocolate, 363
Marilyn's Microwave Peanut Brittle, 252
Martha Washington's Candy, 258
Mel's Saturday Morning Apple Pancakes, 255
Minted Fruit Cordial, 281
Nixon's Baked Grapefruit, 340
Peanut Brittle, 343
Raw Cranberry Relish á la Norvegienne, 248
The Reagan Family Cranberry Sauce, 347
Sour Cream Sauce, 148
Spice Tea, 332
Uncle Ben's Spaghetti Sauce, 253
White House Eggnog, 361–362

Poultry and Seafood

Poultry

Chicken Breasts in Paprika Cream Sauce, 134
Dove on the Grill, 128
Favorite Chicken, 358–359
Grilled Turkey Breast in Pita Pockets, 146
Honey Mustard Chicken, 136
Japanese Chicken Salad, 145
Kadon Manok (Chicken Stew), 141
Kentucky Hot Brown, 151
Korean Chicken, 129
Louisa Adams's Chicken Croquettes, 283
Mexicana Chicken, 132
Poppy Seed Chicken, 131
Roast Wild Duck, 286
Ruby-Red Grapefruit Chicken, 341
Saxby's Quail, 130
Sesame Chicken, 137–138
Thomas Jefferson's Chicken Fricassee, 275

Seafood

Abraham Lincoln's Scalloped Oysters, 296
Favorite Crab Cakes, 149–150
Governor's Fish in Coconut Milk, 140
Great Barbecued Kenai Salmon, 142
Imperial Crab, 135
Pacific Salmon, 139
San Francisco Seasoned Shrimp, 143

Shrimp Curry á la Zephyr Wright, 333–334
Shrimp Scampi, 144
Super Fish, 133
Zachary Taylor's Deviled Crabmeat on Shells, 289

Salads

Abigail Adams's Hot Crab Salad, 273
Barbara Bush's Vegetable Salad, 356
Curried Chicken Salad, 19
Greek Salad, 22
Healthy Cold Turkey Salad, 16
Hot Chicken Salad, 24
Layered Salad, 27
Marinated Vegetable Salad, 20–21
Napa Salad, 25
Orange Chicken Salad, 23
Pasta Salad, 18
Pretzel Salad, 28
Southwest Potato Salad, 26
Summer Rice Salad, 19

Side Dishes

Arizona Baked Beans, 67
Broccoli Casserole, 59
Coleslaw, 61
Creamy Whipped Potatoes, 69
Grandma's Cabernet Risotto, 71–72
Hash Brown Casserole, 65
Hoppin' John, 75
Idaho Potato Lollipops, 76–78
Kenyan Vegetable Curry, 56–57
Kugelis Potato Casserole, 68
LBJ's Pickled Okra, 336
Lemon Yam Puff, 62
Lucy Hayes's Mashed Potato Puffs, 306
Mashed Potatoes, 293
New Potatoes in Burned Butter, 63
Rice and Mushroom Casserole, 64
Sautéed Collard Greens with Garlic and Scallions, 70
Souffléed Corn, 58

Spinach Soufflé, 73
Stuffed Eggplant, Spanish Style, 297
Succotash with Sausage, 344
Summer Squash Casserole, 66
Sweet Potatoes, 74
Thomas Jefferson's Sweet Corn Pudding, 278
Zucchini and Cherry Tomatoes, 60

Soups, Chowders, Stews and Chili

Adam and Eve's Chili, 103
Bacon and Bean Chowder, 35
Burgoo, 48–49
Cape Cod Fish Chowder, 34
Cauliflower Soup, 43
Chicken Chowder, 53
Chili con Carne with Tomatoes, 105
Congressional Bean Soup (Crock Pot), 51
Corn Soup, 305
Curried Pea Soup, 38
Famous Senate Restaurant Bean Soup, 48
Fancy Peanut Soup, 50
Italian Soup, 52
Kay's Shadywood Showdown Chili, 33
LBJ's Favorite Chili, 335
Lentil Barley Stew, 32
Martha Washington's Sherry Crab Soup, 267
Missouri Apple Soup, 40
The Monroes' Mock Turtle Soup, 282
Mushroom Soup, 364
New England Clam Chowder, 42
Oyster Stew, 41
Polish Sausage Stew, 38
Puree Mongol Soup, 330
Ronald Reagan's Hamburger Soup, 349
Santa Fe Soup, 47
Sausage Zucchini Soup, 39
Senator Lincoln's White Chili, 45
Tomato Soup, 52
Tortilla Soup, 30
United States House of Representatives Bean Soup, 31
Vegetarian Chili, 44
Watercress Soup, 37

Politician Index

Bond, Sen. Christopher (*continued*)
    Watercress Soup, 37
    World Series Brownies, 189
    Zucchini and Cherry Tomatoes, 60

Bordallo, Rep. Madeleine Z.
    Governor's Fish in Coconut Milk, 140
    Kadon Manok (Chicken Stew), 141

Boucher, Rep. Rick
    Virginia Brown Bread, 154

Boxer, Sen. Barbara
    Healthy Cold Turkey Salad, 16
    Lemon Blueberry Muffins, 163

Brady, Rep. Kevin
    Chicken Spectacular, 86

Broswell, Rep. Leonard
    Died-And-Gone-To-Heaven Peach Pie, 237

Brown, Sen. Scott
    Chicken Chowder, 53
    Italian Soup, 52

Brownback, Sen. Sam
    Napa Salad, 25

Buchanan, President James
    Mashed Potatoes, 293

Bunning, Sen. Jim
    Mary's Spoon Bread, 155

Burton, Rep. Dan
    Chocolate Melt-Away Dessert, 228

Bush, President George H. W.
    Barbara Bush's Chocolate Chip Cookies, 355
    Barbara Bush's Lemon Bars, 353
    Barbara Bush's Vegetable Salad, 356
    Mushroom Quiche, 354

Bush, President George W.
    Carrot Muffins, 360
    Laura Bush's Hot Chocolate, 363

Mushroom Soup, 364
White House Eggnog, 361–362

Buyer, Rep. Steve
    Summer Squash Casserole, 66

Byrd, Sen. Robert
    Beef Stroganoff, 99
    Favorite Cabbage Rolls, 115
    Pound Cake, 185

Carper, Sen. Thomas
    Broccoli Casserole, 59
    Sweet Potatoes, 74

Carter, President Jimmy
    Peanut Brittle, 343
    Pecan Toffee Tassies, 345
    Succotash with Sausage, 344

Castle, Rep. Michael
    Lentil Barley Stew, 32

Chambliss, Sen. Saxby
    Saxby's Quail, 130

Clay, Rep. William
    Creamy Whipped Potatoes, 69

Cleveland, President Grover
    White Cake and Frosting, 311

Clinton, President William Jefferson
    Chocolate Chip Cookies, 357
    Favorite Chicken Enchiladas, 358–359

Coble, Rep. Howard
    Breakfast "Brains and Eggs," 108
    Oyster Stew, 41
    Sixth District Apple Pie, 241–242

Cochran, Sen. Thad
    Favorite Meat Loaf, 114

Collins, Sen. Susan M.
    Melt-In-Your-Mouth Blueberry Cake, 173

Conrad, Sen. Kent
    Extra Meaty Lasagna, 97–98
    Sunflower Wheat Bread, 157

Coolidge, President Calvin
    Ice Box Cookies, 321

Cornyn, Sen. John
    Texas Pecan Chocolate Chip Pie, 232

Costello, Rep. Jerry
    Homemade Biscuits, 162

Crapo, Sen. Mike
    New Potatoes in Burned Butter, 63

Dicks, Rep. Norm
    Pacific Salmon, 139

Dingell, Rep. John
    Easy But Rich Beef Casserole, 95

Dodd, Sen. Christopher
    Connecticut Yankee Strawberry Rhubarb Pie,
        243–244

Dorgan, Sen. Byron
    Special K Bars, 200

Durbin, Sen. Richard J.
    Hungarian Butterhorn Cookies, 195–196
    Kugelis Potato Casserole, 68

Edwards, Rep. Chet
    Pretzel Salad, 28

Eisenhower, President Dwight D.
    Mamie Eisenhower's Fudge, 329
    Mamie Eisenhower's Pumpkin Pie, 328

Emerson, Rep. Jo Ann
    Cheesecake, 238

Ensign, Sen. John
    Sesame Chicken, 137–138

Enzi, Sen. Michael
    Cheesy Fiesta Dip, 13

Honey Mustard Dressing, 254
    Orange Chicken Salad, 23

Faleomavaega, Rep. Eni
    Island Samoan Chop Suey, 101

Feingold, Sen. Russ
    Lemon Jell-O Cake, 178

Feinstein, Sen. Dianne
    San Francisco Seasoned Shrimp, 143

Fillmore, President Millard, 290

Ford, President Gerald
    Betty Ford's Blueberry Banana Bread, 342
    Ruby-Red Grapefruit Chicken, 341

Gallegly, Rep. Elton
    Giovanni's Pollo Marinato, 102
    Shrimp Scampi, 144

Garfield, President James
    White Loaf Bread, 307–308

Goodlatte, Rep. Bob
    Shenandoah Valley Apple Cake, 169

Granger, Rep. Kay
    Kay's Cookies, 191
    Marilyn's Microwave Peanut Brittle, 253

Grant, President Ulysses S.
    Rice Pudding with Lemon Sauce, 298–299
    Ulysses Grant's Lemon Pie, 300–301

Grassley, Sen. Charles
    Bacon and Bean Chowder, 35
    Carol's Butter Crust, 219
    Cheese Ball, 7
    Cheese Soufflé, 82
    Cocoa Cake, 184
    Lemonade Pie, 217
    Mustard Sauce, 6
    Oatmeal Pancakes, 159
    Polish Sausage Stew, 38
    Pumpkin Torte, 223–224
    Rhubarb Cake, 182

Grassley, Sen. Charles (*continued*)
    Spicy Apple Cookies, 190
    Super Fish, 133
    Swish Pie, 218

Harding, President Warren
    Filet Mignon, 318
    Florence Harding's Almond Cookies, 320

Harkin, Sen. Tom
    Iowa Chops, 122

Harrison, President Benjamin
    Caroline Harrison's Sausage Rolls, 312

Harrison, President William Henry
    Roast Wild Duck, 286

Hatch, Sen. Orrin G.
    Chipped Chocolate Pie, 222
    French Mints, 251

Hayes, President Rutherford B.
    Boston Cream Pie From The Omni Parker
        House, 302–304
    Corn Soup, 302
    Lucy Hayes's Mashed Potato Puffs, 306

Herger, Rep. Wally
    Layered Salad, 27

Honda, Rep. Mike
    Japanese Chicken Salad, 145

Hoover, President Herbert
    Cream Peach Pie, 322
    Girl Scout Cookie, 323

Hoyer, Rep. Steny
    Baked Fruit, 250

Hutchinson, Sen. Kay Bailey
    Kay's Shadywood Showdown Chili, 33

Inhofe, Sen. James
    Mom's English Scones, 210

Inouye, Sen. Daniel
    Fruit Cocktail Cake, 179

Issa, Rep. Darrell
    Pineapple Squares, 202–203

Jackson, President Andrew
    Rachel Jackson's Burnt Custard, 284

Jefferson, President Thomas
    Monticello Muffins, 277
    Thomas Jefferson's Bread Pudding, 276
    Thomas Jefferson's Chicken Fricassee, 275
    Thomas Jefferson's Sweet Corn Pudding,
        278

Johanns, Sen. Mike
    Beef Stroganoff, 109

Johnson, President Andrew
    Stuffed Eggplant, Spanish Style, 297

Johnson, President Lyndon B.
    Ladybird Johnson's Lemon Cake, 337–338
    LBJ's Favorite Chili, 335
    LBJ's Pickled Okra, 336
    Shrimp Curry á la Zephyr Wright, 333–334
    Spice Tea, 332

Johnson, Sen. Tim
    Cherry Nut Bread, 156
    Favorite Cheese Enchiladas, 91–92
    Teriyaki Beef, 118

Kanjorski, Rep. Paul
    New England Clam Chowder, 42

Kennedy, President John F.
    Jackie Kennedy's White House Hot Fruit
        Dessert, 331
    Puree Mongol Soup, 330

Kennedy, Rep. Patrick
    Cape Cod Fish Chowder, 34

Kerry, Sen. John
    Massachusetts Cranberry Bread, 160

Myrick, Rep. Sue
    Tetrazzini, 89

Nelson, Sen. Benjamin
    Ambrosia Fruit and Nut Mold, 236
    Chip Dip, 12
    Coconut Cake, 166
    Nebraska Beef Brisket, 119
    Prime Rib, 120
    Uncle Ben's Spaghetti Sauce, 251

Nelson, Sen. Bill
    Vegetarian Chili, 44

Nixon, President Richard
    Nixon's Baked Grapefruit, 340
    Pat Nixon's Meatloaf, 339

Obama, President Barack
    Crustless Coconut Pie, 208
    Kenyan Vegetable Curry, 56–57
    Michelle Obama's Apple Cobbler, 206–207
    Michelle Obama's Macaroni and Cheese, 80
    The Obama Family's Linguini, 365

Pallone, Rep. Frank
    Raisin Cake (Depression Cake), 186

Paul, Rep. Ron
    Date and Nut Bread, 161
    Texas Sweeties, 192

Pelosi, Rep. Nancy
    Chocolate Mousse, 235

Petri, Rep. Tom
    Raw Cranberry Relish á la Norvegienne, 248

Pierce, President Franklin
    New Hampshire Fried Pies, 291–292

Polk, President James
    Tennessee Ham, 288

Rahall, Rep. Nick
    Hushwee Mediterranean Dish, 106

Rangel, Rep. Charles
    Sautéed Collard Greens with Garlic and
        Scallions, 70
Reagan, President Ronald
    Brandy Whipped Cream Sauce, 349
    Nancy Reagan's Monkey Bread, 346
    Nancy Reagan's Persimmon Pudding, 348
    Pumpkin Pecan Pie, 352
    Reagan's Favorite Macaroni and Cheese, 351
    The Reagan Family Cranberry Sauce, 347
    Ronald Reagan's Hamburger Soup, 350

Reed, Sen. Jack
    Famous Senate Restaurant Bean Soup, 46

Reid, Sen. Harry
    Chicken Breasts in Paprika Cream Sauce, 134
    Strawberry Ice Cream, 229

Risch, Sen. James
    Idaho Potato Lollipops, 76–78

Rockefeller, Sen. Jay
    Baked Apples, 240
    Chocolate Chocolate Angel Food Cake,
        171–172
    Fancy Peanut Soup, 50
    Sunday Brunch Casserole, 94

Roosevelt, President Franklin D.
    Eleanor Roosevelt's Pecan Pie, 325–326
    Franklin Roosevelt's Birthday Cake, 324

Roosevelt, President Theodore
    Clove Cake, 315
    Edith Roosevelt's Fat Rascals (Biscuits), 316

Sanchez, Rep. Loretta
    Garlic Roasted Chicken and New Baby Rose
        Potatoes and Shallots, 85

Schiff, Rep. Adam
    Adam and Eve's Chili, 103

Sessions, Rep. Pete
    King Ranch Chicken, 87

Sessions, Sen. Jeff
    South Alabama Peanut Clusters, 209

Shaheen, Sen. Jeanne
    Chili con Carne with Tomatoes, 105
    Spinach Soufflé, 73

Shelby, Sen. Richard
    Dove on the Grill, 128

Shimkus, Rep. John
    Pork Pie, 113

Skelton, Rep. Ike
    Marinated Vegetable Salad, 20–21

Snowe, Sen. Olympia
    Baklava, 225–226

Spratt, Rep. John
    Jane Spratt's Deluxe Pecan Pie, 212

Taft, President William Howard
    Pumpkin Pie, 317

Taylor, President Zachary
    Zachary Taylor's Deviled Crabmeat on Shells,
    290

Thompson, Rep. Mike
    Grandma's Cabernet Risotto, 71–72

Thune, Sen. John
    Bacon Fried Pheasant, 125
    Sour Cream Chocolate Cake, 188

Truman, President Harry S.
    Bess Truman's Ozark Pudding, 327

Turner, Rep. Jim
    Ann's Chicken Pot Pie, 93

Tyler, President John
    Tyler Pudding, 287

Udall, Sen. Tom
    Biscochitos, 193
    Marge's Chile con Queso Dip, 2
    Tortilla Soup, 30

Van Buren, President Martin
    Charlotte Russe, 285
    Voinovich, Sen. George
    Blitz Kuchen, 213
    German Apple Cake, 168
    Palachinke (Filled Pancakes), 104
    Pork Chops with Apple, 112

Washington, President George
    Cranberry Pudding, 266
    George Washington's Beer, 271
    George Washington's Eggnog, 259
    Martha Washington's Candy, 258
    Martha Washington's Cookies, 262
    Martha Washington's Devil's Food,
    268–270
    Martha Washington's Great Cake, 263
    Martha Washington's Pie, 260
    Martha Washington's Sherry Crab Soup,
    267
    Nelly Custis's Recipe for Hoecakes,
    264–265
    Shrewsbury Cakes, 261

Waxman, Rep. Henry
    Favorite Cake, 174

Wicker, Sen. Roger
    Chicken Casserole, 84
    Poppy Seed Chicken, 131

Wilson, President Woodrow
    Tea Cakes, 318

Wolf, Rep. Frank
    Applesauce Cake, 170

Young, Rep. Don
    Moose Swiss Steak, 116

States Index

Souffléed Corn, 58
Summer Rice Salad, 19
Sweet and Sour Meatballs, 9–10
Tailgate Hero Sandwich, 83
Watercress Soup, 37
World Series Brownies, 189
Zucchini and Cherry Tomatoes, 60

MONTANA
Huckleberry Pie, 215–216

NEBRASKA
Ambrosia Fruit and Nut Mold, 236
Beef Stroganoff, 109
Chip Dip, 12
Coconut Cake, 166
Nebraska Beef Brisket, 119
Prime Rib, 120
Uncle Ben's Spaghetti Sauce, 253

NEVADA
Chicken Breasts in Paprika Cream Sauce, 134
Sesame Chicken, 137–138
Strawberry Ice Cream, 229

NEW HAMPSHIRE
Chili con Carne with Tomatoes, 105
Spinach Soufflé, 73

NEW JERSEY
Honey Mustard Chicken, 136
Raisin Cake (Depression Cake), 186

NEW MEXICO
Biscochitos, 193
Marge's Chile con Queso Dip, 2
Tortilla Soup, 30

NEW YORK
Congressman Peter King's Lemon Squares, 211
Sautéed Collard Greens with Garlic and Scallions, 70

NORTH CAROLINA
Breakfast "Brains and Eggs," 108
Oyster Stew, 41
Sixth District Apple Pie, 241–242
Tetrazzini, 89

NORTH DAKOTA
Extra Meaty Lasagna, 97–98
Special K Bars, 200
Sunflower Wheat Bread, 157

OHIO
Blitz Kuchen, 213
German Apple Cake, 168
Grape Dogs, 124
Palachinke (Filled Pancakes), 104
Pork Chops with Apple, 112
Southwest Potato Salad, 26

OKLAHOMA
Mom's English Scones, 210

OREGON
Tomato Soup, 54

PENNSYLVANIA
New England Clam Chowder, 42

RHODE ISLAND
Cape Cod Fish Chowder, 34
Famous Senate Restaurant Bean Soup, 46

SAMOA
Island Samoan Chop Suey, 101

SOUTH CAROLINA
Jane Spratt's Deluxe Pecan Pie, 212

SOUTH DAKOTA
Bacon Fried Pheasant, 125
Cherry Nut Bread, 156
Favorite Cheese Enchiladas, 91–92
Sour Cream Chocolate Cake, 188
Teriyaki Beef, 118